# Good Earth
## Home & Garden

D0128936

All Purpose
Tub, Tile
...ee Cleaner

Published by

# Krause Publications

700 E. State St.
Iola, WI 54990-0001
Telephone 715-445-2214
www.krause.com

Please call or write for our free catalog of publications. To place an order or obtain a free catalog, please call 800-258-0929, or please use our regular business telephone 715-445-2214.

Library of Congress Catalog Number: 2001096284
ISBN: 0-87349-341-9

Neither the publisher nor author can be held responsible for any injuries, losses, or other damages resulting from the use of information in this book (due to different conditions, tools, and individual skills); however, great care has been taken to ensure that the information in this book is accurate.

Mother Nature illustration by Gary Carle.

# Dedication

This book is dedicated to my mother-in-law, May Kellar. Through the years, my mother-by-marriage has developed into a special friend. May often supplies our family with newspaper and magazine articles she has found here and there. She likes to share ideas and information she has gleaned from the local gardeners' clubs and extension groups to which she belongs. Plant starts and clippings from her greenhouse often find their way to my garden. Her enjoyment of gardening and trying both new and old, inexpensive solutions around the house are infectious, and gave me the "bug" … thanks, Mom. Oh, and thanks to my husband, Byron, for having his mom. (Or was it the other way around?)

## To my kids and grandkids:

Moments at home and in your garden are precious, quiet times that help to calm your spirit so you can focus on the simple joys in life; they can be perfect opportunities to take stock of your life. Cleaning and tending your garden and your home can remind you to also clean the dust from the edges of your mind and soul, and clear out the unneeded "baggage" of your life. Time spent doing the simple chores of nature and home will help you define yourself and your real priorities.

—My love to all.

# Acknowledgments

Sunny Trapp: RainShadow Labs employee, for helping me prepare for the photo shoot.

Beverly Buffington: RainShadow employee who keeps my grammar and spelling in check.

My son, Justin Kellar, who helped prepare some of the recipes for the photo shoot and who is always willing to give me a helping hand when I really need it.

My husband, Byron Kellar, for his patience with me; and for always taking on these "extra" projects; and for always dropping everything and running to my side whenever I yell, "Help!"

Columbia County Extension Service

Scappoose Oregon Garden Club

Christine Townsend: my editor, for her help and support.

Ross Hubbard: the primary photographer of this book.

# Table of Contents

INTRODUCTION

CHAPTER 1: BEAUTIFYING AND CLEANING SOLUTIONS FOR THE HOME 10

*Interiors 12*
All-Purpose Wall, Tub, Tile, and Counter
   Cleaner 13
Cleaning Ceilings 13
Super Spotless Mirror and Window Cleaner 14
Cleaning Fireplaces 14
Fabric and Upholstery Cleaner 14
Wood Cleaning and Polishing Oil 15
Leather Clean and Shine 15
Leather Moisturizing Polish 15
Degreaser 16
Vacuum Fresh 17
Dry Carpet Cleaner and Revitalizer 18
Paint Remover 18
Home Air Freshener 19
Baby Room Anti-Dust Spray 19
Mother's Disinfectant Spray 20
Disinfectant Spray #Two 20
*Garage/Shop and Home Exteriors 21*
Clean Up and Organize Ideas 21
Controlling Moss on Your Roof 21
Moss Cleaner for Wood Decks 21
Bleach for Concrete Walks 22
Special Grease Spot Remover 22
Tile and Siding Cleaner 23
Pool and Spa Cleaner 23

CHAPTER 2: ENERGY EFFICIENT, FUEL SMART—SIGNS OF THE TIMES 24
Home Insulation Tips 26
Cost-Saving Car Facts 28

CHAPTER 3: EXPECT THE BEST, BUT THINK LIKE A SCOUT:
PREPARE FOR DISASTERS 30

First Aid Kit 32
Safe Disposal of Old Chemicals 33

CHAPTER 4: ALL CREATURES GREAT AND SMALL 36

*Making Treats for Your Pets 39*
Healthy Doggie Treats 39
Dog and Cat Hot-Weather Treats 40
Kitty Goodies 41
High-Protein Bird Treats 42

*Pet Problems and Solutions Around Your Home 43*
The Fussy Eater 43
The Ears 43
Skin Problems 44
Digestive Upsets 45

*Natural Remedies for Happy, Healthy Pets 46*
Health Tonic for Your Cat or Dog 46
Super Odor Remover for Real Emergencies 46
No-Lick Spray 95
Dry Pet Shampoo 47
Flea and Bug Repellent Gentle Shampoo for Pets 48
Flea Repellent Bed 48
Toothpaste for Pets 49
Fur Conditioner for Your Pets 50
Cat Box Deodorizer 50

*Gifts for Pets and Their Owners 51*
New Puppy Gift Set 51
Christmas or Birthday Gifts for Dogs 51
All-Purpose Cat Basket 52
For Our Fine-Feathered Friends—and Bird Lovers,
Too 53

# Chapter 5: Taking It Outdoors 54

Gardening: What's in a Name? 56
The Unusual Yet Functional Garden 57
My Favorite Herbs 58
Edible Flowers 60
Vegetables 63
Eatable Garden Layout 64
Creative Containers 65
Starting with Seeds 66
Potpourri from Your Garden 67
Floral, Herb, and Citrus Spice Potpourri 68
French Lavender Potpourri 68
More Fun with Plants 69
Herbal Vinegars, Butters, and Teas 70

# Chapter 6: Functional Garden Basics 72

Homemade Soil Mixes 74
Casey's "Super Natural" Basic Potting Soil Mixes 74
For Heavy Clay Soils 75
For Sandy to Normal Soils 76
Fertilizers, Composts, and Mulches, Oh My! 77
Compost 77
Mulches 78
Fertilizers 79
Fishy Fertilizer 79
Seaweed Fertilizer 80
Coffee and Berry Mash Fertilizer 80
Herbal Mold Inhibitor 81

# Chapter 7: Mother Nature's Solutions for the Garden and Pests 82

Garden 84
Shine and Glow Houseplant Polish 84
Natural Weeding Solution 85
Mold and Mealy Bugs on Plants 85
Fungus Stopper 85
Mildew-Mold Control for Plants 86
Garden Chemical Neutralizer 87
Natural Weed Deterrent 88
Pests 89
Natural Pest Control 89
Garden Fly Trap 89
Natural Roach Killer 89
Homemade Insecticide 90

Aphids-Be-Gone! 91
A Good and Pretty Bug 91
Aphid and Beetle Repellent 91
Yellow Jackets' Death Trap 92
Softening Bees 92
Byron's Slug Fighter #One 93
Byron's Slug Fighter #Two 93
Other Tricks to Rid Your Garden of Slugs 93
Fly, Tick, and Mosquito Repellent Spray 94
General Bug Spray/No-Lick Spray 95
Controlling Spiders 95
Mother Nature to the Rescue 95

**Controlling Larger Pests 96**
Birds 96
Old Fashioned Deer and Rabbit Repellent 96
Quick and Easy Deer and Rabbit Repellent 96
Moles and Mice 97
Mole-Away 97
Skunks, Rats, Rabbits, Raccoons, and Opossums 98
Dogs and Other Family Pets in the Garden 99

# CHAPTER 8: HOMEMADE GIFTS FOR NEWLYWEDS, HOUSEWARMINGS, AND YOURSELF! 100

**For the Home 102**
Housewarming Gifts: Say It with Fragrance! 102
For the Mr. Fixit Who Has Everything 102
Spring Cleaning Basket 102
Herbal or Floral Gifts from Your Garden to Your Kitchen 103
    Tinctures 103
    Jellies 103
**For the Garden 104**
Gardener's Pail 104
Painted or Stenciled Clay Pot 105
**Additional Garden Gifts 106**
Potpourri Basket for the Crafter 106
Byron's Slug Safari Basket 107
Decorated Wooden Potpourri Box 107
A Starter Herb Garden 107
Floral or Herbal Jellies 107
Herbal Vinegars 108
More Homemade Gift Ideas 109

INDEX 110-111

# Introduction

## ABOUT THIS BOOK:

Homes and gardens—these are topics that just keep coming back year after year, because our homes and gardens are where we nurture our families and ourselves. They are where we gather with our friends to give of ourselves, and at the same time, where we spend our quality, alone time. Our homes are our sanctuaries, our escape from the rest of the world.

For most people, a garden—whether it is a few containers on the back deck, or a full acre of flowers, plants, or vegetables—is a place of quiet beauty. Gardens are places to commune with Mother Nature and enjoy her beauty, fragrance, and health-giving harvest. Working around the home can also be a primary joy, if you open your heart to it. In today's rush-rush world, home can be where you shut off outside stimuli and derive joy from concentrating on simple tasks, or a place to give yourself a break. Many times, if you also listen to soothing or enervating music while doing household or gardening duties, that break turns into a pleasant "get-away."

Many people worry about using pesticides, and so will not even attempt to plant a garden. Some see gardening as too work-intensive. I hope that this book will give you easy and fun solutions for some of the frustrations of gardening, as well provide some ideas for pesticide-free, beautiful, usable gardens.

Blending beauty and function is always a win–win situation.

# Chapter 1

# Beautifying and Cleaning Solutions for the Home

# In this Chapter:

## *Interiors*

All-Purpose Wall, Tub, Tile, and Counter Cleaner
Cleaning Ceilings
Super Spotless Mirror and Window Cleaner
Cleaning Fireplaces
Fabric and Upholstery Cleaner
Wood Cleaning and Polishing Oil
Leather Clean and Shine
Leather Moisturizing Polish
Degreaser
Vacuum Fresh
Dry Carpet Cleaner and Revitalizer
Paint Remover
Home Air Freshener
Baby Room Anti-Dust Spray
Mother's Disinfectant Spray
Disinfectant Spray #2

## *Garage/Shop and Home Exteriors*

Clean Up and Organize Ideas
Moss Control for the Roof
Moss Control for the Deck
Concrete Cleaner
Grease Spot Remover
Tile and Siding Cleaner
Pool and Spa Cleaner

*W*hether you get that cleaning bug in the spring or the fall, at some point most of us roll up our sleeves every once in a while and say—"That's it! I *really* have to clean." We know we want to save money and take control … so here we go! Get your rubber gloves handy and let's make cleaners that are natural, and environment-friendly.

There are several safety rules that I want to cover with you first before heading into this chapter. I have given you some easy-to-make formulas for cleaning solutions in your home. I use baking soda and vinegar quite a bit, as they are safe when used alone or in the following formulas. It is important to note that as  much as it may seem like a good idea to combine bleach with vinegar or ammonia to make a stronger cleaning compound, **do not do it!** Bleach, when combined with vinegar (without other buffers) produces a *toxic* fume and boils a poisonous brew, so do not mix them (this warning includes any toilet cleaners or other cleaners that may contain bleach). Even though I usually encourage creativity, you must be careful when it comes to mixing chemicals!

"Safety first" should always be our motto; this book emphasizes natural and safe formulas. Even though the formulas made here are much gentler than their commercial counterparts, you still need to store them out of the reach of pets and children. Make sure to label your homemade compounds along with the date you made them (see Chapter 3, page 34). With just a little effort, all your commercial chemicals and homemade concoctions will be labeled and dated, just like your medicines, and you will easily be able to manage them. It feels so good to take control and organize your items around your home.

# All-Purpose Wall, Tub, Tile, and Counter Cleaner

I know we could have probably cleaned something in the time it took to say that title—but you will use this cleanser a lot. This is your all-in-one, handy-dandy home cleaner that you will use over and over again. It is safe for the environment and safe for you. The baking soda and vinegar are the workhorses, but the tea-tree and witch hazel are naturally light antiseptics to give you an antibacterial edge, plus they help clarify the formula so it wipes up cleanly.

You can add a few drops of essential oil or fragrance if you like, to fragrance your home as you clean (I like to add one drop cinnamon and one drop clove so that when I get done cleaning, it smells like I have been baking—without the calories).

## You will need:

1/2 cup water
1/2 cup baking soda
1/2 cup white vinegar
1 teaspoon tea-tree extract or tincture (tea-tree oil will do in a pinch, but then you will need to shake the bottle occasionally)
1/4 cup witch hazel

Mix together and keep in a spray bottle (will last several months). Use this to clean your kitchen appliances too!

## ✨ Cleaning Ceilings ✨

To clean ceilings, use the All-Purpose Cleaner, but to make it easier, use a paint roller and a sponge mop. First, use the paint roller, put a small amount of cleaner on the roller, and "roll on the cleaner." Afterwards use your sponge mop (dipped in water then rung out) to go over the area to remove the cleaner and the dirt! With the long handles this makes the job easier (you can also do this on washable wall surfaces). Put a towel around the handle and leave a little bunched up around the top of where your hands are on the handle, and you will catch any drips running down your handle (there should not be much if you are using small amounts of cleaner and remembering to wring out the sponge first).

# Super Spotless Mirror and Window Cleaner

Use this spray on your mirrors and windows, and then wipe off the mix and polish with a crumpled newspaper. Wow! The shine and clarity are so wonderful, now you can ask, "Mirror, mirror on the wall … "

*You will need:*

1/2 cup water
1/2 cup white vinegar
1/4 cup isopropyl alcohol

Mix this together and keep in a spray bottle; it will keep for several months.

## Cleaning Fireplaces

Use this mix to remove the soot on glass fireplace doors and on the brick surrounding the fireplace opening. Spray on, let sit for one hour and have a cup of coffee or tea, come back and use newspapers to wipe off the soot from the glass.

Make a mix of 60 percent white vinegar and 40 percent water.

# Fabric and Upholstery Cleaner

*You will need:*

1 teaspoon baby shampoo
1 teaspoon glycerin
1/8 cup isopropyl alcohol
2 cups water

Mix this together and test on a small area of the fabric to be cleaned. This works on a wide variety of stains on fabric furniture. It also makes a good pre-wash treatment for spots on clothes. This formula will store for many months.

# Wood Cleaning and Polishing Oil

To take great care of your wood furniture, you need to use a polish that will clean and shine, yet will not leave a film on the wood. Here is my favorite wood cleaner and polisher for furniture, wood railings, or wood floors.

### You will need:

4 ounces raw linseed oil
3 ounces turpentine
1 ounce of beeswax
1 teaspoon of olive oil

Melt the beeswax slowly in pan on the stove (leave the heat on low as this kind of wax can be flammable at high temperatures). Do not leave unattended. Once the wax is melted, remove from heat and stir in the linseed oil first, then continue to stir and add the other ingredients one at a time. Stir until blended, and pour into a bottle. Apply it to the wood surface by pouring some on a soft rag and buffing it in. Wow—shine without grime!

# Leather Clean and Shine

### You will need:

1/4 cup baby shampoo
1/4 cup isopropyl alcohol
2 cups water

Mix together the ingredients and buff leather with soft rag (or a spare sock with no mate) to clean leather furniture or car seats. It does not take very much to clean the leather (this will work on vinyl surfaces too). Follow with the moisturizing polish.

# Leather Moisturizing Polish

### You will need:

1 teaspoon neat's-foot oil
3 tablespoons olive oil

Heat the neat's-foot oil to soften it if needed, and then mix these two oils together. It will clean off any remnants of the homemade Clean and Shine formula, and give your leather moisture to protect it from cracking. Buff until all the oil is removed or absorbed into the leather.

## Degreaser Formula

### You will need:

1 teaspoon citrus (lemon or orange) essential oil

1/2 cup isopropyl alcohol

This will cut grease in ovens, on pots and pans. Mix and store in spray bottle. Make sure that when you clean the oven that it is off, and the kitchen well ventilated.

## Vacuum Fresh

Take a couple of tablespoons of vermiculite or perlite (used in the garden chapter, page 72) and put in the center of an old hankie or a square of scrap fabric. Add a few drops of essential oil or fragrance oil to the vermiculite, and then pull up the corners of the fabric. Tie them together with a ribbon to make a sachet. Toss or pin this sachet in your vacuum cleaner bag, and freshen the air while you vacuum your house. You can also toss these in your sock drawers or other drawers to "freshen" them up. I like to hang one in my closet on a hanger—and I have even made one with cedar essential oil mixed with a little vanilla fragrance, to store with my sweaters during the summer to repel moths (smells much better than mothballs).

Mother Nature says: "Always label your homemade products, and if you want your life to be really easy, put the recipe on the label too; when you run out you can make up more without looking for the recipe again!"

## Dry Carpet Cleaner and Revitalizer

### You will need:

1/4 cup baking powder
1/4 cup cornstarch
1/8 cup arrowroot powder

Sift together and store in a cheese shaker. For new liquid spills standing on top of a Scotchgarded® fabric surface, just toss on the powder and wipe up. To lift old "dried on" stains, add just enough water to make a paste. Apply to the fabric; let it sit forty-five minutes or so then brush with a stiff-bristled brush, then vacuum.

## Paint Remover

Ever find a beautiful antique someone has painted at a garage sale? There it sadly stands, with chipped and peeling paint. "Too bad," you say … but wait: why not take it home, remove the paint, refinish it, and make it shine?

There are lots of great books on refinishing furniture, but what I have to offer is a list of ingredients you can mix yourself to help with the process.

### You will need:

4 ounces of benzoil
2 ounces of isopropyl alcohol
2 ounces of acetone
1 teaspoon wax shavings

Melt the wax and then mix the rest of the ingredients together. This is a caustic mix, strong enough to eat through the wood, so do not leave it on the wood for more than twenty minutes. For heavily-painted surfaces, use a paint scraper or a razor blade in a blade holder. Do not dig at a piece (which will damage the wood), but instead remove the old paint using a light, vertical motion. If the paint is lightly applied and comes up easily, use stainless steel scrub pads.

Place the removed paint on newspaper, and dispose of safely.

Use only on the painted parts as it will work as a solvent on the paint. Only use it in a well-ventilated area. Remember to keep it away from pets and kids. Use gloves, and label it; keep in garage. This Paint Remover will be good for eighteen months or so.

When the paint is removed, you are ready to sand, putty, and stain your new piece (your hardware store will help you with directions and the tools you will need for this stage of the process).

## Home Air Freshener

This is a quick-to-make, quick-to-work spray air freshener.

### You will need:

1 cup vodka
20 drops of your favorite essential or
    fragrance oil

Blend this together and do not drink! Put in a cute little spray bottle and mist in the bathroom or other places that need freshening.

## Light "Baby Room" Anti-Dust Spray

This light cleaner leaves nothing toxic behind—the oil and baby shampoo help clean and dissolve grime as well as the alcohol, which is lost to evaporation in short order. And best of all, it is safe for you, and safe for baby.

### You will need:

1 tablespoon avocado oil
1 tablespoon isopropyl alcohol
1 tablespoon baby shampoo
1 cup water

Mix together, put in a bottle, and use with your rag when doing light dusting—this will help clean general surfaces.

# "Mother's" Disinfectant Spray

Mother Nature's natural disinfectants go to work in this formula—just combine them, shaking the bottle before each use and spray. I often take this and add 1/2 cup of isopropyl alcohol, then fill a bottle for my purse (this makes a great waterless hand disinfectant/ cleaner that really works).

## *You will need:*

1 teaspoon tea-tree oil
1 cup witch hazel

# Disinfectant Spray #2

This will help reduce germs even if it will not totally disinfect. I like this formula for diaper pails, pet areas and to refresh garbage cans.

## *You will need:*

1/2 cup chlorine bleach
1/2 cup isopropyl alcohol
7 cups water
8 drops lemon essential oil
8 drops tea-tree oil

Mix together and keep in a spray bottle.

# GARAGE/SHOP AND AROUND THE HOUSE

## Clean Up and Organize Ideas

These areas are often forgotten and, if neglected, can detract from some of the wonderful effects of your clean and beautiful home and garden. Heavy-duty challenges present themselves in these particular areas, so here are some heavy-duty solutions!

## Controlling Moss on Your Roof

Moss is a type of plant growth that prefers damp, shady locations—usually on the north sides of trees and roofs, and on roofs that have a lot of trees hanging over them. (If you are from Arizona, you can probably go on to the next formula!)

### You will need:

1/2 ounce copper sulfate
1 gallon of water

Spray on roof with a tank sprayer, and let it sit for ten minutes or so. Rinse with pure water. This formula is great on everything but metal roofs, eaves, and downspouts, but you can still use it on three-tab and wood roofs even if you have metal eaves—just rinse the metal parts with pure water right away when you are done with the roof. If you have a metal roof, moss is not usually a problem; if it is, buy zinc-galvanized flashing and put these strips at the top of your roof to discourage moss growth.

You can use the above also to remove moss from concrete.

## Moss Cleaner for Wood Decks

### You will need:

1/2 cup water
1/2 cup lemon juice (fresh-squeezed)
1 cup white vinegar

Mix all together. Use a tank sprayer or plant mister to spray on the area. Let it sit for forty-five minutes and then rinse with water. This will loosen the moss and you can scrape it off. Applying this cleaner also discourages moss regrowth.

# Bleach for Concrete Walks, Concrete Patios, and Concrete Garage Floors

### You will need:

- 2 tablespoons liquid dish detergent
- 1 tablespoon chlorine bleach
- 1 tablespoon baking soda
- 2 cups water
- 3 drops cinnamon or citrus (orange or lemon) essential oil

Add chlorine bleach to water first, then dish detergent, baking soda; add the essential oils last. Scrub this mixture on the area of the stain and let sit overnight. Hose off in the morning. Keep children and pets away from the area until rinsed.

# Special "Grease" Spot Remover for Concrete

On a heavily stained concrete area, just apply several drops of the "pure essential oil" of cinnamon, orange, or lemon on that area, and let sit overnight. Hose off in morning, keeping children and pets away until you do. Make sure you are not using *fragrance oil* or *flavoring*, as neither will work as well. *Essential oils*, on the other hand, are caustic and will eat right through grease!

## Tile and Siding Cleaner

This formula is slightly abrasive, so do not use it on your shiny indoor tile; it is meant for outdoor siding and porous outdoor tile.

### You will need:

3 cups warm water
3 teaspoons of liquid dish detergent
3 tablespoons baking soda
2 tablespoons borax

Mix all together and wash down outside tile and/or house siding with it.

## Pool and Spa Cleaner

Sometimes grime and excess spa and pool chemicals build up on the edge of the pool and create rings. If you do not want to drain the pool to clean away the rings, just whip up some of this mix and scrub around the edges. If you only use a little, it will not throw the pH off.

### You will need:

1/4 cup gentle baby shampoo
1/4 teaspoon borax
2 teaspoons baking soda
1 teaspoon isopropyl alcohol

Mix all together and scrub the stain around the pool or spa using just a small amount of mix and a toothbrush or other soft brush.

# Chapter 2

# Energy Efficient, Fuel Smart — Signs of the Times...

# In this chapter:

Home Insulation Tips
Cost-Saving Car Facts

When I originally planned this book, this chapter was not in it. Recently, we have seen a real rise in fuel and energy prices leaping far above the standard rates for inflation. Now, *everyone* is concerned about how to spend less on these items. So I asked my husband Byron (a handy guy to have around) to help me put together this chapter on how to get back to the basics of energy efficient homes.

When Byron and I were just starting out (we have been married 25 years), we faced these same concerns with energy—everything is cyclical, isn't it? Together, we did some research, then put together this list.

How do we use energy in the United States? According to several university studies, below are ranges of the percentage of power used across the United States. These are averages and can vary by location.

Home Heating 56–58%
Water Heating 13–16 %
Refrigerator and Freezer 4.5–9%
Air Conditioning 3–5%
Cooking 4–6%
Lighting 4–6%
Television and Computers 3-5%
Clothes Drying 1.5–2.5%
Miscellaneous 1–2.5%

# Insulate Your Home and Save

Since home heating and cooling represents 59-62 percent of the energy costs in your home, this is where you can realize the most savings. Insulation will keep your home warm in the winter and cool in the summer. Insulation materials create a "dead-air space" that slows down the air transfer from outside to inside.

To stay warm in the winter and decrease your home-heating bill, what you want to accomplish is to keep the cold air from getting in your house at its bottom. Stop drafts and provide good insulation in your floors and walls. To keep the warm air from escaping from the roof, install good ceiling insulation, and circulating fans to move the heat downward again. All these measures work the same way in hot weather, too, so that when you use your air conditioner, the insulation traps the cold air inside and keeps the warm air out.

Some power companies will check your home and make suggestions as to how you can make it more energy efficient. Often they will do this at no charge to you, and some even give "credits" if you use this service, because you are working cooperatively toward the same goal—less power usage through more efficient use of energy.

Insulating your home is an obvious start. When building, this is easy, but not so easy on some older homes. Check with a professional company that can give you an estimate of what you can accomplish now.

# Here Are Some Other Things That You Can Do to Help Insulate Your Home:

Make doors and windows airtight. If you can see daylight around your doors or windows when they are closed, repairing them will save many energy dollars. You may need to re-set door hinges to get a better fit, but if the space is fairly small you may get by with weather stripping. Weather stripping should last three to five years and can save you a lot of money. There are several kinds of weather stripping available, but the easiest is the adhesive-backed stripping. Make sure surfaces are clean and dry; pull off the tape backing, and smoothly and evenly apply. Reinforce with small tacks spaced every five inches or so.

You also may want to install a door sweep on the bottom of the door. A sweep fits where the door meets the door frame at the bottom of the house.

For windows and sometimes doors, you can also use caulking to seal up cracks—then paint the caulking to match your door frame or walls.

## More Money-Saving Tips for Conserving Energy around Your Home:

* In the winter, snug up a drafty door by rolling up a throw rug and placing it against the bottom of door frames on windy nights (remember cold seeks low points to enter the house).

* Close your blinds and curtains when it gets really cold at night to help keep heat in. In the summer, close them first thing in the morning when the house is cool to help keep heat out.

* Turn down the thermostat in winter when you go to bed—use grandma's comforter instead!

* During the day, dress warmer and lower your thermostat a few degrees to save money.

Make sure your heat thermostat is clean and working correctly. Also, check to see if it is in a draft, which will make your furnace work longer and overheat your home.

If you have radiators, clean them regularly. Dirt can cover and block the flow of air around the radiator.

Do not block heating/cooling vents with furniture or other items.

If you have a large house and are not using all the rooms, turn off the heat to the areas not used.

If you do not have storm windows, double insulated windows, or energy efficient windows, and are on a budget, buy thick, clear plastic and make your own "energy efficient" windows by covering the outside of the window. Stretch the plastic tightly and staple to frame with staples every two to three inches. This will create "dead-air" space insulation for your windows, and you can still see out.

Check to make sure all your vents to the house are functioning properly and insulated. Ceiling vents are critical, as they can lose a lot of heat from your house and increase your bill.

Check the vent/damper in your fireplace as well—close it when it is not in use.

Wear warm socks and clothes in winter. Watch television cuddled up under a blanket. You will feel warmer,

Mother Nature Says: "Using less fuel is food for the environment."

and you'll save money too!

If you are in an area that cools down on summer evenings, turn off the air conditioner and open the windows.

Use the exhaust fan in your kitchen to help warm air to escape from your home when you are cooking in the summer.

On hot days, make salads and barbecue outside so you do not add extra heat to the house.

Clean your air conditioner and check the filter at the beginning of every season. If it is clogged, it will run longer than necessary. Make sure to clean the filter and/or replace it often.

Run your laundry at night when heating and/or cooling systems can be turned down.

Dress cool! My husband Byron is always too warm and I am always too cool (a seemingly universal problem between men and women). I love wearing sandals and being barefoot in summer, but I noticed Byron would have socks and tennis shoes on. I convinced him to start wearing shorts and sandals, too; and now I can turn back the air conditioner a bit for my comfort and cost savings. The moral to this story is: Dressing according to the season or weather is sometimes a very simple—and comfortable—way to save money.

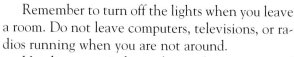

Remember to turn off the lights when you leave a room. Do not leave computers, televisions, or radios running when you are not around.

Use dimmer switches to lessen the wattage used at dinner and for other "marginal lighting" events.

Eat by candlelight at least one night a week; not only is it romantic, it will save you money. (I have found this a great way to get a guy with a cost-effective mindset into the "romantic" spirit.)

Use the higher wattage of light bulbs where you need them most for reading or seeing critical items. Use lower wattage bulbs in halls or other areas where light is not so critical.

Instead of keeping a porch light on, use timers and motion sensors outside as they only come on when you need them.

Replace incandescent bulbs with florescent or other "energy efficient" lighting.

Put light-colored (white or cream) shades on your lamp instead of dark shades, which "block" the light.

There are some automobile maintenance things you can do yourself to save money:

Change the oil; dirty oil = lower performance.

Check the fan belt; if it is too tight, your engine is working too hard and is not fuel-efficient.

Snow tires use a little more gas; take them off your car when you do not need them.

Check spark plugs; clean them or replace if needed.

Plan your trips. We live six miles from a small town and twenty-five miles from Portland, Oregon. We make a list of everything we need before we go shopping in either town. Also plan what you will need to take with you when you go so that you do not play "Keystone Cops," having to return several times to get everything, wasting precious time and gas.

# More Fuel Hints ... Byron's Tips on Saving Money with Your Automobile:

Cars are an integral part of life for most Americans. They not only transport us, but for some, they symbolize "who we are." Some cars are sporty, some functional, and others even luxurious. But whatever they are, they also are *expensive*.

Here is a list of things Byron and I thought of that can save money where cars are concerned. One way is to have your car running at peak efficiency. The other is to maximize your time in the car so you do not waste precious (and expensive) fuel.

Cost-saving car facts:

* The heavier your car is, the more it costs to run: consider buying a lighter, fuel-efficient vehicle.

* Using cruise control on long trips can save money.

* Do not "rev" your engine at stop signs, when starting an engine, or before shutting it off—revving burns more gas and increases engine wear.

* When possible, take your bike, the bus or mass transit, or carpool.

* When on the road, travel when the rest of the "crowd" is not—early mornings or late evenings. You will experience less stall-time in traffic, which, of course, burns more gas.

* Roll down the windows when possible for cooling the car. The heater and the air conditioner lower the "miles per gallon" you are getting from the gas in your car.

* You can easily get 15 percent more miles-per-gallon if you take care of your engine. Make sure you get regular tune-ups.

# Expect the Best, But Think Like a Scout: Prepare for Disasters

# IN THIS CHAPTER:

First Aid Kit
Safe Disposal of Old Chemicals

I am far from what I would call an "alarmist." I am positive about the future, but at the same time, I consider myself to be a realist—maybe because we live in the country and are surrounded by tall trees that occasionally fall and take out a power line for a day or so. We have had an occasional snow or windstorm with similar effects. So, I think it prudent, whether you live in the city or the country, to uphold the Scouting motto: "Always be prepared." So, what does that mean? Well, you should always have a few "emergency" supplies on hand.

Do you remember the story of the ant and the grasshopper? The little ant worked all day long getting ready for hibernation in the fall, while the grasshopper played his fiddle and played all day long. When fall came, and the cold wrapped around the grasshopper, he almost froze to death because he had no shelter or food to eat. The little ants were warm in their shelter with plenty to eat. One little ant took pity on the grasshopper and brought him in because his music gave him great joy, and the grasshopper promised to be better prepared in the future.

I am like the ant—always organizing and planning—but I also love grasshoppers. No matter which you are, you must plan for the unexpected … because it *happens!* Just as you take out car insurance or life insurance to protect yourself and your loved ones, you need a little household emergency kit as insurance, too. It does not need to be expensive or take up a lot of space.

Mother Nature says: "Learn from the ant and the grasshopper."

# So What Do We Recommend?

Here is a list of some of the very basics that everyone should have.

A small first aid kit containing:

    Antibacterial spray

    Ace bandages

    Ointment

    Adhesive bandages

    Scissors, tweezers

    Large gauze pads and tape

    Syrup of ipecac

    Eye wash

    Tea tree oil

    Witch hazel

    Sweet oil

    Cold tablets

    Basic pain medication (over the counter)

    Cough syrup

    Anti-diarrhea medication, indigestion and motion sickness medications

Candles (a couple of dozen small, medium, and large candles)

Matches

A week's supply of canned foods that can be eaten without cooking (open and serve)

Extra blankets

2 to 3 flashlights and extra batteries

A battery-operated radio

Some money ($50.00 or so for an emergency, stashed securely in your home)

Enough gas in a gas can to get you a short distance (five to ten gallons)

Enough bottles of water for one week (drinking water, water to make food, baby formula, wash dishes, and help flush toilets if necessary)

The above list gives you the bare minimum, but will make a big difference to you and your family in an emergency, so I urge you to gather them all together. If you need to budget, just buy an extra item each shopping trip to put away. If you have babies, I would suggest adding one week's supply of formula

and diapers to the basics list. And, do a check of your items every year to see if anything needs to be used or replaced.

We tend to think that disasters, like storms, power outages, or earthquakes just won't happen to us. I hope they don't! But consider the old adage: "If you are prepared for the worst, the worst doesn't happen." Preparedness is cheap insurance. Plus, you will feel more secure knowing that you are ready and able to take care of yourself and loved ones if needed.

If you live outside of town, like we do, and can have storms that can take out power for a week, you might want to consider adding these to your list:

Additional food, water, and gas

A personal generator and fuel

A propane cooker (for outdoor use only) with a few small propane bottle refills

A deck of cards, books you have not read, or a non-electric game or two to amuse yourself until the power comes back on.

## Safe Disposal of Old Chemicals

In the garage and around your home you will pile up a considerable amount of useless and unwanted chemicals. It might be time to take inventory of all your chemical items. If you have had household chemicals for more than two years, you may want to consider getting rid of them.

Even though you are environmentally conscious and considerate, and make your own, safe products, it is likely you will purchase some toxic chemicals, or have old chemicals lurking about under cupboards and in the garage. Look around your garage or garden shed and round up any and all unused chemicals, including herbicides, pesticides, commercial fertilizers, used motor oil, and get ready to have a chemical "clean up" day. When it comes to handling all these chemicals, you will need to arm yourself with tools for personal protection.

## Assemble Prior to Tackling This Project:

Heavy gloves

A paint mask to lessen the effects of inhalants

Full clothing (like an old jogging suit, cover-all—make sure your arms and legs are covered)

Sensible shoes—no sandals, please!

Safety goggles

## Okay, Here We Go:

**1.** Suit up. Take a box at a time around your house, garden, and garage, and collect all commercial chemicals for sorting. (Make sure they are tightly lidded or capped to avoid accidentally mixing them or splashing them on yourself.)

**2.** Assemble all chemicals in a well-ventilated area on an old (or covered) table, and start sorting.

**3.** First, sort all the chemicals that you believe to be more than two years old. Any that you can remember purchasing recently, label with your best guess of the date of purchase. (When you buy chemicals in the future, always use an inexpensive white label and put the date of purchase on the bottle or can—there is a unwritten rule that you should use these types of materials within two years of purchase.) Get rid of all old chemicals; put them in boxes labeled "Discard."

**4.** Continue sorting all chemicals until you have three sets of labeled boxes: "Garden," "Garage," and "Household" chemicals.

**5.** Take all the chemicals you are keeping, and store in a cool, dry place, out of the reach of children and pets.

**6.** Now, pack the chemicals to discard neatly in boxes (making sure you have no open containers). Transport them in the back of your truck, or in the trunk, away from people.

**7.** Do not put chemicals in plastic bags; they may break and cause a hazard.

**8.** Keep children and pets away from your sorting and transport areas.

**9.** Do not smoke or stand near heaters or electrical equipment during any of this process.

**10.** Most communities have a "Chemical Clean-Up Day" on which you can turn in your household chemicals. Or you can call your local dump, extension service, or city sanitation department and they will guide you to a hazardous-waste disposal site near you.

**11.** Keep all chemicals in original containers if possible. If they are missing labels, then label what you think they are.

**12.** Never mix products together.

**13.** Make sure everything is sealed; transfer any leaking products to secure, labeled containers.

Mother Nature Says: "Never pour these products down the drain, or put them in with the regular trash; doing so could create a hazard for people, pets or the environment."

# Pets: All Creatures Great and Small

# IN THIS CHAPTER:

## Making Treats for Your Pets

Healthy Doggie Treats
Dog and Cat Hot-Weather Treats
Kitty Goodies
High-Protein Bird Treats

## Pet Problems and Solutions around Your Home

The Fussy Eater
The Ears
Pets' Skin Problems
Pets' Digestive Upsets

## Natural Remedies for Happy, Healthy Pets

Health Tonic for Your Cat or Dog
Super Odor Remover for Real Emergencies
Dry Pet Shampoo
Flea and Bug Repellent Gentle Shampoo for Pets
Flea Repellent Bed
Toothpaste for Pets
Fur Conditioner for Your Pets
Cat Box Deodorizer

## Gifts for Pets and Their Owners

New Puppy Gift Set
Christmas or Birthday Gifts for Dogs
All-Purpose Cat Basket
For Our Fine-Feathered Friends—and Bird Lovers Too

Our pets provide companionship in our homes and gardens. Pets become part of the family, don't they? They love us unconditionally and are loyal and true friends.

In a day when people carefully read the ingredients in their foods, cosmetics, and body care items because of federal regulations, we are also becoming concerned about the chemicals used in our pet care products.

Sometimes, the old techniques and remedies are still the best help for our animal friends, but there are a lot of good *new* ideas and trends, too. Today, all sorts of new ideas, products, and services for pets are emerging: Huge pet centers and stores, pet cemeteries, pet day care, pet sitters, pet products, pet

clothes, computer pets, and more. In an age of computers and cocooning, our relationships with our animal friends are even more necessary to keep balance in our lives. My husband and I have four pets: two large dogs, a tiny "house dog" and one large cat. Since our children have grown and moved away, our pets have become our next generation of "kids."

This chapter is dedicated to our pets. We have included products used in helping pets with pests (some of the recipes can be used by humans too), treats, and home remedies for your pets! We like to give a "welcome-home" pet gift any time a friend of ours gets a new pet.

# Making Treats for Your Pets

## Healthy Doggie Treats

Here is a nutritious snack for your pooch. Birds like them too; just leave the ground crackers and oats a bit larger so they can pick them out.

*You will need:*

1 cup ground crackers
3/4 cup ground oats
1 tablespoon soy powder
1 cup bacon drippings
1 tablespoon peanut butter

Grind up the crackers very finely. Melt the bacon drippings and stir the peanut butter into the warm drippings. Now add the ground crackers, oats, and soy powder. Press this mixture into a pan. When they have cooled completely, cut into squares, or roll into balls. If your batch is too firm, add a little more bacon drippings the next time you make it. To make the batch firmer, just add more ground crackers.

# Dog and Cat Hot-Weather Treats

Mix up the following and pour it in plastic ice cube trays with your pet's name on them!

## You will need:

1 cup water

2 tablespoons of beef or chicken bouillon

1 finely chopped hot dog (or 3 table-spoons tuna fish or chopped chicken gizzards)

Heat the water and dissolve the bouillon in it. Set aside and let cool for a while. When cool, pour the liquid into each of the ice cube compartments. When done, spoon a little of the chopped hot dog (or choice of meat) into each of the compartments.

Cover, then label and store in freezer. Now, when the weather is warm, your dog or cat will not beg to share your ice cream (which isn't good for them, anyway). Instead, you can give them their own icy treat for those hot, "dog-days." If you are worried your pet's tongue will stick to the ice cube, just run a little water on the cube before serving.

Here are more frozen treat ideas:

Drain off the liquid from moist dog-food cans.

Drain off the liquid from water-packed tuna cans.

Use the old beef broth from leftover stew.

# Kitty Goodies

Do you think your cat is finicky? In a twitch of a cat's brow, you can have these healthy cat treats made and ready for a gourmet offering.

## You will need:

- 1/2 cup chicken broth
- 4 ounces plain yogurt
- 1 seven-ounce can tuna fish (drained; save the water the tuna is packed in for "Fishy Fertilizer," page 79)
- 3 slices whole wheat bread, crumbled
- 4 canned herring fillets (drained) and chopped into bits

Put the broth into a small bowl. Add the bread-crumbs and plain yogurt, and stir until all the liquid is absorbed. Now, add the tuna fish and chopped herring; stir until smooth. Refrigerate the mixture for a couple of hours, or until it is firm. Cut into squares or roll into balls (butter your hands when making the balls, cats like the taste of butter, too). You can control the softness or firmness of this recipe by adding or taking away breadcrumbs.

# High-Protein Bird Treats

### You will need:

1 cup of bacon drippings or other solid
   kitchen fat
1-1/2 cups breadcrumbs
1-1/2 cups millet
1/4 cup sunflower seeds
1/2 cup peanut butter
1/4 cup rolled oats

Melt the fat in a saucepan until softened; remove from heat. In a separate bowl, combine the remainder of the ingredients and mix. Now, add the dry goods to the "softened" fat (which should be partially set-up) and stir thoroughly.

Spread the mix onto small wood slabs and hang from a tree, or put the mix in a disposable tin foil pan and poke four holes to make corners and hang with wire from a tree, or use a pine or fir cone and spread the mix in and around the cone and hang that for the birds (great for outdoor birds or indoor birds).

## The Fussy Eater

Sometimes a bored or nervous pet appears to be a fussy eater. Here are some ideas that may help.

1. Serve different brands/flavors of food at least three nights a week.

2. Remove any extraneous stimuli such as loud noises, kids, and other animals from the area when food is served.

3. Use the Health Tonic on page 46 on food to help stimulate an interest.

4. Add warm water to the food to help release the aroma to make it more appealing.

5. Add a little garlic or onion powder to the food to bump up the flavor; hey, it works for us doesn't it?

## The Ears

Ear problems in pets usually occur in the form of fungal or bacterial infections, mites, fleas, or foreign objects.

**Ear Mites:** Wipe out your pet's ears with a 50-50 blend of apple cider vinegar and water; it repels mites and keeps dogs' ears clean and fresh. Next, wipe out the ear with oil from a vitamin E capsule to help promote healing.

**Yeast Infection of the Ears**: You can get yeast medications from your veterinarian, but my pet's groomer actually helped me save money with this suggestion. Use human vaginal yeast cream (sold over the counter in most states). Put a small amount on a tissue, and rub in your pet's ears.

# Pets' Skin Problems

There are a few things you can do to calm down irritated skin and "itchy" spots, but one is to bathe your pet in colloidal oatmeal shampoo or soak (you can find this at your pharmacy or health food store). "Colloidal" just refers to the size of the oatmeal, as it is very small and easier to use as well as faster-acting. Oatmeal is very soothing to the skin and will calm down hot spots. You can also use a small amount of calamine lotion, if you suspect it is a bug bite in a place where your pet will not lick. Milk will also help calm down skin irritations, and is non-toxic if your pet licks it. Another way is to apply some unscented, uncolored glycerin-based lotion on the area (again to calm down and sooth the area). Yet another is to apply "sweet oil" (which is refined olive oil) to the area. The sweet oil not only will help soothe irritations, but it gives the pet's coat a shine, and you can use the opportunity of the oil application to give your pet a "massage" with a little oil—which your pet and you will both find soothing—and it will reassure and calm your pet (nervousness being a possible contributing factor to the skin condition, to begin with). Alternate the above treatments with the application of a little witch hazel from time to time, as it will help cool the "hot spots."

**Dandruff:** Crush an aspirin and add the crushed aspirin and 4 drops tea tree oil to every 1/2 cup water to make a dandruff rinse for use after shampooing. Pour over pet and use your fingers to work into skin. Let sit one to two minutes, then rinse.

**Fleas:** Make your pet distasteful to fleas, and up their B vitamins at the same time! An old-fashioned way is to add brewer's yeast to your pet's diet—one to two teaspoons of powdered brewer's yeast, and maybe a few shakes of garlic powder (dogs like garlic too, and so do some cats). Fleas also do not like the herbs thyme or rosemary. Fleas do not like citronella or cedar, either.

But since, with the above remedies, we are not killing the fleas because we want to resist using pesticides, what can be done? Well, Byron has another hint for us! After you make or buy your dog's cedar bed, one night, put a bright light and a large pan or tray of water down low, near the dog bed. Fleas are attracted to the warmth of the light, so they will jump toward the light out of curiosity, and land in the pan of water under the light and drown.

**Mange:** This skin condition is completely different from hot spots. When your pet is scratching and the hair is falling out and has a bad smell, your pet may have mange. If it is severe or wide-spread, call your vet. If it has just started, you can sometimes deter and even stop it by buying an over-the-counter lime-sulfur combination available at your pet or feed store (one is called Lymdyp®; it is safe and effective). You will probably have to repeat the process two or three times to get it all (remember to also treat your pet to an oatmeal shampoo or sweet oil treatment to help soothe the poor pet as well).

**Antiseptics:** My recommendations are on the natural side: tea tree oil or witch hazel applied directly (both are available at your drug store). For cats, use only witch hazel as tea tree products can be harmful to them.

**Ticks:** These nasty little "blood suckers" can cause diseases such as Lyme disease and Rocky Mountain spotted fever, so we do not want them around! Here are some natural ways to rid your pet of ticks. Try garlic! Add a little garlic to your pet's food; it actually makes your pet distasteful to fleas and ticks.

If you need to remove a tick, this is what I recommend. Get a pair of tweezers, some Q-tips, and a pair of rubber gloves. Put on the gloves and arm yourself with the tweezers. Calm your pet and get her to lie down (or get someone to help hold your pet). The old farmers used kerosene to do this; I prefer tea tree oil or Tabasco sauce applied generously with a Q-tip to the back end of the tick. When the tick backs out, grab it in the middle with the tweezers and destroy the tick (usually you can just pop them with the tweezers), and put it down the drain or toilet. Never just "pull out" the tick, as it will break in two, leaving the front still working in your pet, which can cause infection.

## Pets' Digestive Upsets

**Constipation:** Add a little olive oil to your pet's food (1/2 teaspoon to a tablespoon) depending on the size of the animal; this will provide lubrication and get things moving.

**Diarrhea:** I'm not sure who this is hardest on—the pet or the owner! My vet says it is okay to give your pet a little Kaopectate® to help stop the flow. Go easy though: Kaopectate contains a clay that helps absorb the excess liquid in the bowel and stabilizes the condition; too much and your pet has other problems! I also give my pets Pedialite®, which is available at drugstores. Intended for babies, it replaces electrolytes lost through diarrhea and makes pets and people feel better. (I carry some in little packets when traveling in Mexico or other countries, and it helps us to recover faster.)

**Bad breath:** Put a few drops of liquid chlorophyll in their drinking water, and it will help clean your pets from the inside out, freshen their breath, and supplement their diet. Parsley is a natural breath cleaner; I offer a small amount to my dog when I'm eating it (and she is interested in *everything* I eat).

# Natural Remedies for Happy, Healthy Pets

## Health Tonic for Your Cat or Dog

You want to see shiny coats, bright eyes, and wet noses? This vitamin tonic will do the job! Mix 1 teaspoon a day with their food to add more nutrients. The greens help stop the cravings to eat grass for vitamin A, the garlic detoxifies their systems, and the oils give shine to their coats.

### You will need:

1/4 cup cod liver oil
1/2 cup water
1 cooked garlic clove
1 teaspoon chopped fresh parsley
1 tablespoon vegetable oil

Finely chop the cooked garlic clove and fresh parsley, then add all the ingredients together and keep in an amber bottle in the fridge. Shake well prior to each use. Do not exceed more than 1 teaspoon per day.

## Super Odor Remover for Real Emergencies

Did your pet come in contact with something that smells nasty, and a regular shampooing didn't help? Follow these four steps to remove the worst of odors.

Put white vinegar in a spray bottle and spray down your pet (do not get in eyes—yours or your pet's). Then bathe using our Flea and Bug Repellent Gentle Shampoo; dry thoroughly.

Then use straight baking soda as a dry shampoo; brush out. Spray your pet with pineapple fragrance mixed with water (6 drops of oil to 1/4 cup water); keep shaking as you are spraying—this will even remove skunk odor.

## No-Lick Spray

See page 95.

# Dry Pet Shampoo

How does a dry shampoo work? It takes excess body oil and dander out of the coat. As a touch up for dogs or for cats (who usually hate water) this is an easy-to-make dry shampoo. Sprinkle a little on, then just brush out the powder, oil, and grime from your pet's coat.

### You will need:

1/2 cup baking soda
1/4 cup corn starch
1/4 cup rice flour
3-4 drops of your favorite essential oil or fragrance (my poodle always smells like a little peach)

# Flea and Bug Repellent Gentle Shampoo for Pets

### You will need:

1/2 cup baby shampoo
5 drops citronella essential oil
3 drops lemon fragrance oil
3 drops rosemary essential oil
3 drops thyme essential oil

Mix together and use on pets; it will repel fleas and other pests, and your pet will smell clean. Most shampoos contain harsh detergents, which are not needed to get your pet's coat clean and shiny. Baby shampoo is gentler. It will clean, but not promote "hot spots."

# Flea Repellent Bed

Make a cedar bed with heavy-duty fabric and cedar shavings. Inside the bed add a few sachets made from the following:

### You will need:

6 drops rosemary essential oil
6 drops thyme essential oil
1 cup vermiculite

Add the 12 drops essential oils to the vermiculite and make a few small sachets to stuff into the pillow. These sachets can be used elsewhere also to discourage fleas. Just add some cedar shavings to the sachet mix and stuff these anywhere you have a flea problem. Refresh the pillow occasionally by adding a few drops of essential oils listed above to the fabric of the bed.

# Toothpaste for Pets

I know this may sound like a bit *much*, but many animals do not get enough "roughage" in their food to help clean the tartar off the teeth as nature intended. Occasionally brush your pet's teeth, or when your pet has terrible breath and you can see it is coming from his yellowed teeth. It will clean and polish his teeth and is non-toxic. Now, if we could just get them to cooperate!

## You will need:

1 teaspoon baking soda
1 teaspoon calcium carbonate
2 teaspoons milk of magnesia
1 teaspoon glycerin

Mix together to make a paste and use a soft toothbrush to brush your pet's teeth. Make up a fresh batch whenever needed.

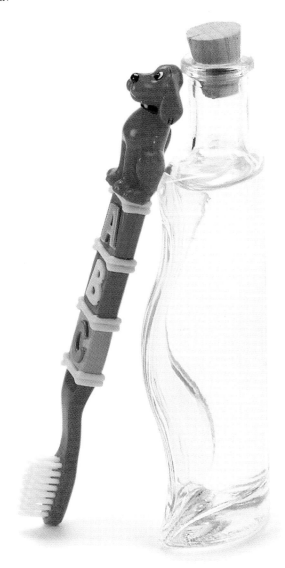

## Fur Conditioner for Your Pets

### You will need:

2 cups cold water
1 ounce baby shampoo
1 egg yolk

Beat the egg yolk and then combine it with the other ingredients. After shampooing, massage this mixture into pet's fur and let sit for one minute. Rinse out with warm water. This is a great conditioner—the egg yolk conditions, the cold water adds shine and the shampoo rinses it out. You can add a drop or two of fragrance or essential oil to the conditioner if you wish.

## Cat Box Deodorizer

Add this mix to commercial cat box litter to help keep kitty's box smelling fresher.

### You will need:

2 cups baking soda
3 cups vermiculite
3 drops lemon fragrance

Blend together. Use 1 cup of this mix for every 4 cups of cat litter. The lemon fragrance freshens the room; the baking soda helps remove ugly cat odors and, along with the vermiculite, absorbs moisture.

# GIFTS FOR PETS AND THEIR OWNERS

## New Puppy Gift Set

This is a lovely and caring gift to give someone with a new pet. Bringing a new pet into your home is much like bringing home a new baby—there is so much work and so much pleasure! Let your friends know that you acknowledge this special new addition to their family.

### You will need:

Small-sized homemade Flea Repellent Bed, page 48
No-Lick Spray, page 95
Doggie Treats, page 39
Chew toys

## Christmas or Birthday Gifts for Dogs

Our pets are a part of our family, too, and don't want to be overlooked. We have three dogs: "Mad Max" is a German shepherd, "Meshia" is a Chow mix, and "Katie" is our 4-pound pocket poodle—and they *all* love treats! Make a basket for each pet in the family and put a personalized tag on it. Our pups seem to understand Christmas morning and look for their treats under the tree—and in their Christmas socks!

### You will need:

Doggie Treats, page 39
Gentle Shampoo, page 48
Dog toys and a doggie brush

# All-Purpose Cat Basket

Cats are independent and loving all at the same time. We have one named "Walker" (he is part Siamese, and when he was young he would jump and "walk" on everything). Walker would love this basket!

### You will need:

Dry Pet Shampoo, page 47
Kitty Goodies, page 41
Cat Box Deodorizer, page 50
Cat toys

# For Our Fine-Feathered Friends—and Bird Lovers, Too

A basket with a birdhouse or a make-your-own birdhouse kit, homemade bird treats and a bird toy or mirror make a clever basket! We do not have a bird, but it is fun to make the bird treats and "hang" them in trees, and watch our wild friends feast!

*You will need:*

Bird Treats, page 42
Birdhouse or kit
Bird toys

# Chapter 5

# Taking It Outdoors ...

# IN THIS CHAPTER:

Gardening: What's in a Name?

The Unusual Yet Functional Garden

My Favorite Herbs

Edible Flowers

Vegetables

Eatable Garden Layout

Creative Containers

Starting with Seeds

Potpourri from Your Garden

More Fun with Plants

Herbal Vinegars, Butters, and Teas

For many people, the outdoor areas of their homes bring every bit as much satisfaction as their indoor areas—and maybe just a little more enjoyment. When the weather is great, we naturally want to be out in it. I love to work outside in my garden. Where I live, the spring and summer seasons are short, and I spend as much of those seasons outside as possible. My husband has even attached a greenhouse to our home so I can extend my gardening pleasure as long as possible. When we added a spa to the addition, I was pleasantly surprised to learn that the heat and moisture provided by the spa created a great environment for my plants; everything thrived.

In this chapter, I have included recipes and formulas for tackling a range of outdoor challenges from cleaning to controlling bugs. You'll also find some inexpensive, natural solutions for patios and garden walks that quickly solve annoyances, allowing us to get back to the very important task of *enjoying* our outdoor space!

# Gardening: What's in a Name?

When you look at most flower and herb books, there are usually many Latin names that are difficult to understand. Why are the formal names of most plants not only difficult to pronounce, but also apparently unhelpful in determining a plant's identity? For example: the *Echinacea Purpurea* is the same thing as a purple coneflower; a *Chrysanthemum Maximum* is a Shasta daisy … and we could go on.

There are so many varieties/species of each flower or plant such as a "daisy" or "peppermint," that a formal Latin word for each one is the only way we can be sure we are all talking about the same one. Okay; but "Why Latin?" you might ask. We can thank Carl Von Linne, a Swedish doctor in the 1700s for creating a uniform system for naming plants. Latin is considered the root language for many of the world's languages, so when naming or communication disputes arise in science, we fall back on Latin as something with which we can all agree. As a matter of fact, in the year 2000, the FDA mandated that all botanicals listed in personal care products must be identified by their Latin names (be looking for larger labels on your products to accommodate this), so that we consumers can research these products and be better informed about what's in the package.

# The Unusual Yet Functional Garden: Explore Eatable Landscaping!

Ornamentals are beautiful and functional, and I do love them, but there are so many books on simple gardening that I am not going to spend a lot of time on them. This book is about solutions to many of our home and garden needs, but I cannot resist spending a little time on a passion of mine—edible plants for your garden that you can also work into your landscape designs. Edible landscaping is a way to grow vegetables, herbs, fruits, berries, nuts, flowers, and some ornamental plants in harmonious groupings without

the use of dangerous chemicals. Vegetables, fruit and nut trees, and berries come to mind for all of us when the word "eatable" garden is mentioned. Instead of going into great depth about these, I am going to focus on my very favorites: herbs and edible flowers.

Edible landscaping is not only fun to plant and eat, but when you look at your work, whether in the ground or in a container garden setting, you will get personal satisfaction knowing you have created a garden that will nourish your eyes, soul, and your stomach. You can enjoy your creation in wonder and good health.

The reasons to plant edible landscapes are many: The variety of foods you can provide for yourself while saving money are among the most important. But consider, too, how you can improve your health by growing your own foods naturally, and the independence that comes with the gardening skills your ancestors cultivated. What about the real synergy you can experience when you work with Mother Nature? And what better place to spend quality family time than in a garden?

Edible landscapes can have a broad range of influences beyond beauty and good health. Some plants can lure pollination bees, and some can be used in homemade concoctions to repel pests. Some plants can improve the soil, block the wind, and give you shade.

# MY FAVORITE HERBS

**Rosemary** (*Ros marinus*)

With beautiful green-gray, skinny aromatic foliage, rosemary is a hardy, tall plant with many uses. Rosemary can grow to 3 or 3-1/2 feet tall, and does well in containers. Rosemary will thrive in less-than-perfect soils, and likes to completely dry out between waterings.

**Oregano** (*Origanuum vulgare*)

Make sure the variety you get is really oregano and not marjoram. Oregano has a stronger flavor than marjoram, and has more heart-shaped leaves. Usually the flowers are soft pink. It grows to a height of about 1-1/2 feet. Although it is most commonly used in Italian cooking, the oil of pure oregano has recently shown promise as a cosmetic with many health benefits.

**Thyme** (*Thymus vulgaris*)

Pass some time with thyme ... this short, bush-like herb bears pink or white flowers on thin, silvery foliage. Clip this herb often, and use thyme with chicken. (I love rosemary-, thyme-, and garlic-herbed chicken.) There are many varieties of thyme, such as lemon, caraway, and lavender thyme. This is a very aromatic herb that grows 4- to12-inches high, depending on the variety.

**Marjoram** (*Majorana hortensis*)

As already mentioned, this herb is related to oregano (sometimes people think they are buying dried oregano when they are really buying marjoram). Marjoram is a compact bush that grows to about 1-1/2 or 2 feet, and can be grown in pots. It has a delicate flavor,

and is often used to flavor fish, tomato, and pasta dishes. Marjoram's white or pale pink blooms attract bees. Marjoram likes rich soil and full sun.

**Mint** (*Mentha*)

There are many members in the mint family and I love all of them. Mints are great contained in pots, as their roots are real creepers and can take over a whole garden. Mint goes well with lamb, makes delicious tea, and is an aromatic, invigorating addition to your bath. Peppermint is also really soothing to upset stomachs. I like to plant traditional peppermint and spearmint along with chocolate or pineapple or ginger mints and more. Most mints will grow up to about 2 feet.

**Sage** (*Salvia officinalis*)

There are a few varieties of sage, all beautiful, and they sport a variety of leaf and flower colors. I like to combine the flavors of lemon and sage in cooking. Sage is generally very hardy but requires full sun and well-drained soil. It grows to approximately 2 feet in height.

**Dill** (*Anethum graveolens*)

This is an attractive annual that grows fine, wispy foliage and interesting yellow flowers with a strong scent. All parts are edible and rich in vitamins. Combine some fresh dill with onions in watered down vinegar for a flavorful snack. Dill grows a little over 2 feet, in dry, sunny locations away from winds.

### Tarragon (*Artemisia dracunculus*)

This herb has long, narrow leaves and seems to be odor-free until it has been cut. This herb is also used in cooking fish, chicken, stuffing, salads, and more. Tarragon requires a sunny location, well-drained soil, and protection from wind. Grows to approximately 2 feet.

### Basil (*Ocimum basilicum*)

This is a striking plant that can grow to 2 feet high. Basil requires warm and sunny positions. Most basil is suitable for drying and is fairly hardy. Once you try it, chances are you will fall in love with basil, and you will want some in your garden every summer.

### Chives (*Allium schoenoprasum*)

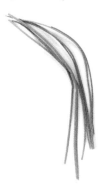

Chives is one of my favorite herbs. I take little clippings from it regularly for seasoning food. When it goes to seed, it grows wonderful, large clover-like flowers. Chives grow in large clumps to heights of about 1 foot (if you divide them occasionally).

### Garlic (*Allium sativum*)

Garlic is an ancient plant used for many purposes. In stories and myths, it is used to ward off vampires, but in reality we use it for seasoning and good health. Strong and pungent, much research has gone into studying garlic's possible abilities to ease asthma, lower cholesterol, inhibit blood clots and more. Garlic has green tops and white bulbs that can be split and planted for more, or eaten. Garlic likes full sun and grows up to one foot.

### Parsley (*Petroselinum crispum*)

Great for eating (iron-rich with lots of vitamins, and it's a natural breath purifier) and easy to grow, parsley is another one of my favorites! There are many kinds of parsley.

### Chamomile (*Anthemis nobilus*)

Chamomile can grow between 1 to 2 feet high and has dainty, thin foliage with small, daisy-like flowers from which you can make herbal tea. It is a delicate-looking and fragrant herb that is sometimes used as a ground cover.

### Bay (*Laurus nobilus*)

This is a shrub that was cherished by the ancient Romans for both culinary and decorative purposes. It will grow into a small tree if you do not manage it. Rich, green leaves give excellent flavor to stews and soups. It is hardy in most soils, but it is slow to grow.

### Chervil (*Anthriscus cerefolium*)

The Romans introduced chervil to England. It is a low growing, 1-foot tall annual. This herb has very delicate foliage and dainty white flowers, and is sometimes used as a ground cover just like chamomile. Chervil prefers semi-shade. Like basil, it is not quite as widely known but is worth trying.

### Horseradish (*Armoracia rusticana*)

Called "monk's mustard" in ancient times, the flavor of the grated root to this clump-like plant is very strong. The roots are harvested once a year, but can never be entirely removed. Like onions and chives, horseradish thrives in moist soil.

Mother Nature Says: "Be more like a bunny; have some flowers for lunch."

# EDIBLE FLOWERS

In Victorian times, eatable flowers were all the rage. Why not create a lovely "potpourri" in your tummy? Here are some flowers that are tasty and fun:

**Nasturtium** (*Tropaeolum*)
This flower has beautiful foliage that can be green or marbled green-and-cream. The leaves are delicious in salads. The flowers, in colors like red and yellow and peach, are eatable (with both a light texture and taste) and look great in salads. Smaller varieties grow to about 1 foot tall, but climbing varieties grow to greater heights. Nasturtiums can be cross-planted with tomatoes (the climbing variety will wind around tomatoes but not overpower the plant—it will look like an unusual tomato plant with flowers and fruit).

**Calendula** (*Calendula*) **(pot marigold) and Marigolds** (*Tagetes*)
Colors of off-white, orange, or yellow work great in foods. Calendula grows up to 2 feet and is fairly hardy. These plants also help repel certain insects. The Lemon Calendula (*Tagetes tenuifolia*) has a citrus-like flavor.

**Note: French Marigolds are *not* edible—check with a garden master or extension group to make sure that the variety you have is eatable; when they are, they are a treat!**

**Borage** (*Borago officinalis*)
The leaves, when cooked, will remind you of spinach. Borage is hardy and prefers full sun. Pinch back the leaves on a regular basis to keep the plant under control. This flower blooms small, blue flowers that are edible, too.

**Roses** (*Rosa*)
Despite the thorns, rose flowers are beautiful and sweet to eat (only the blooms are edible). In Victorian times, candied (sugared) roses were often used decoratively on foods. Rosewater and glycerin softened our great-grandmothers' skin, and rose teas were the vogue. Roses come in a wide variety of colors and sizes. Baby bushes, climbers, and full-size shrubs are available.

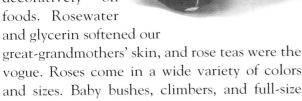

**Sunflowers** (*Helianthus annuus*)
The flowers are not eatable, but the seeds that fall from them late in maturity are delightful!

## Ideas for Using Eatable Flowers:

Dry the eatable flower and lightly coat with egg whites and dust with sugar; eat like candy or use as summer cake decorations.

Freeze in ice cubes and put this lovely, decorative ice in punch bowls or in glasses of iced tea, lemonade or other summer drinks.

Make floral vinegars, tinctures, or teas.

Mother Nature Says:
"Not all the flowers
pictured are edible:
some are just 'eye-
candy.' Double-check
before you snack!"

# GARDEN VEGETABLES

I wanted to mention these vegetables because I have grown them virtually anywhere: in containers in and around the house, in gardens by themselves and in combinations with herbs and eatable flowers for a beautiful and functional garden.

**Tomatoes** (*Lycopersicon esculentum*)
There are all sorts of new tomato hybrids, in a variety of sizes, shapes, and colors. I think these look great in the garden. Although they need lots of water, once they start producing, it is likely that you will harvest plenty.

**Peppers** (*Capsicum frutescens or Capsicum annuum*)
Like tomatoes, there are many hybrids of peppers, and most of these plants are low growing, beautiful, and produce lots of peppers.

**Kale** (*Brassica oleracea acephala*)
In shades of red, green, white, pink, and purple, this plant must be one of the most dramatic and beautiful of all ornamental vegetables. Kale is low-growing and looks like an ornamental plant, but you can harvest the leaves for salads or cooked vegetable dishes. Kale is regarded as a winter vegetable and can stand cooler weather.

**Lettuce** (*Lactuca sativa*)
Many varieties are available and I can keep lettuce going from May to November in my region (with two plantings). Lettuce is a cool-weather crop. Clip the leaves down about halfway a couple times a week, and the leaves just grow back. When the weather gets warm, shade the lettuce and provide lots of water at night.

**Spinach and Chard** (*Spinacia oleracea, Beta vulgaria cicla*)
These are also cold-weather crops and I treat them just like lettuce. By cutting the tops off and eating just the tops, I manage to keep the crop going for quite some time by forcing additional plant growth.

**Onions**(*Allium cepa*) **and Chives**
Cut off the tops of the plants and keep them going for a long time.

**Cucumbers** (*Cucumis sativus*)
This plant grows very large—but I have grown them in large containers, and just one plant can produce lots of cucumbers!

**Brussels sprouts** (*Brassica oleracea gemifera*)
These take a long time to mature, but they are one of the most decorative of the "sprouts" family. They often grow in winding spirals, or straight columns, and look wonderfully decorative in the back of a garden—and, of course, you can eat the sprouts.

# EATABLE GARDEN LAYOUT

If you do not have enough outdoor space to plant a traditional garden, you can have clever container gardens all together on a deck, or just a few placed around your home or apartment. How about one or two on the front porch, and one on the deck, or even several placed inside in your sunniest windows? There is always a way to grow a health-giving garden, no matter where you live.

## Sample Garden Layout

Remember to leave "easy access" walk-through areas
so you can tend and pick your garden

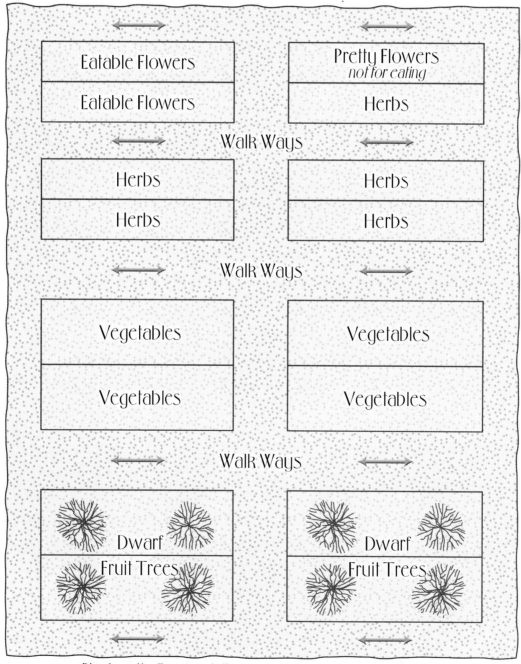

| Eatable Flowers | Pretty Flowers *not for eating* |
| Eatable Flowers | Herbs |

Walk Ways

| Herbs | Herbs |
| Herbs | Herbs |

Walk Ways

| Vegetables | Vegetables |
| Vegetables | Vegetables |

Walk Ways

| Dwarf Fruit Trees | Dwarf Fruit Trees |

Plant pretty flowers, tulips and daffodils at base of fruit trees.

# CREATIVE CONTAINERS FOR YOUR GARDEN

You do not have to spend a fortune on classic clay pots or plastic containers for your plants. Be creative with your container garden! Here are some alternative containers as suggestions; use your creative process to think up others. Just remember to cut holes in the bottom for drainage.

An old, 55-gallon drum cut in half

An old tire

An old, wooden carpenter's box or gun box

A chipped china urn

A hollowed log or piece of driftwood

An old pot

A picnic basket

An old cowboy boot or work boot

An old wheelbarrow or red wagon

An unused fountain

## Start with Seeds

Have you seen those seed strips sold in garden stores? These are made to help you with your seed spacing while in the garden, but you can make your own for a fraction of the cost. Here's how: Get a roll of toilet paper and roll out a long strip. Place the seeds the correct distance apart on the toilet paper (the seed packet will tell you; spacing varies with types of seeds). Now fold the toilet paper over with the seeds in the middle. With a fine mist sprayer, spray water on the toilet paper (just dampen lightly; do not soak). Let the seed strip air dry, and then plant as needed. One-ply toilet paper is fine if you handle it carefully, two-ply is easier. If you want to speed up seed propagation, mix in a little powdered, unflavored gelatin to the water before spraying it on the folded toilet paper—gelatin works as a gentle fertilizer to help start your seeds.

## Special Seed Starter Plant Mix for Indoor Seed Starts

Mix equal amounts of peat moss and perlite or vermiculite to make a blend. Then plant your toilet paper seed strips, and water well. Keep soil moist until small starts sprout. When the weather is good and the plants are an inch or two tall, transplant to outside soil or containers.

# Potpourri from Your Garden

I love to save some of the summer floral and herb garden to enjoy through the winter months. If you have leftovers from your eatable garden that you have not consumed and want to preserve, this is a great way to bring your garden indoors for the winter.

Botanical mixtures have long been of interest to homemakers and lovers of nature's beauty. The ancient Egyptians and Greeks would throw fresh floral mixtures in front of processions, and in and around the great banquet halls. They used fragrance blends to develop cosmetic preparations and perfumes. Through the Middle Ages, flower, herb, and root blends were used as cures and to improve the smell in dank, dark places. Many of the old recipes were written down, and family blends were handed down through the generations. Many of the recipes from this era are fraught with detailed, complicated processes involving hand selecting flowers, particular harvest times, and how to dry, blend, and store the potpourri. I hope this chapter simplifies the process. Many basic garden flowers can be used to make potpourri, and the recipes I have given can be changed to accommodate the particular flowers grown in *your* garden.

Some of the more common garden flowers used in potpourri blends are roses, lavender, geraniums, violets, lilacs, hydrangeas, orange blossoms, honeysuckle, marigolds, mums, statice, and baby's breath. Actually, any flower that has a fibrous texture is suitable for drying.

For best results, always pick the flowers fresh, and start the drying process right away. Use silica (available in craft stores) for delicate flowers. Many hardy (fibrous) flowers will dry hanging upside down by clothes pins on a line. If you pick fresh flowers and start the drying process immediately, the preserved colors will be better than when you start with an aged, cut flower.

After the flowers are totally dry, treat them with a fixative such as orris root, gum benzoin, or a commercial fixative found at craft stores. Spray lightly with fragrance and put in a closed container to "cure" for a few days, and you now have potpourri. The fun part is combining different dried flowers for textures and color combinations to match your room décor. Potpourri is lovely placed in decorative bowls and dishes around your house. Potpourri can also be made into wreaths, sachet balls, or used around the base of a winter floral arrangement. Here are a couple of my favorite potpourri recipes.

# Floral, Herb, and Citrus Spice Potpourri

# French Lavender Potpourri

1 cup lavender
1 cup red or pink rose petals
1/2 cup chamomile
1/2 cup dried lemon verbena
1/2 tablespoon powdered gum benzoin
1/2 tablespoon powdered or crushed orris
   root

Follow the same directions given for the Floral, Herb, and Citrus Spice Potpourri.

## You will need:

2 cups dried rose petals
1 cup dried rose geranium leaves
1 cup rosemary needles
2 tablespoons each of ground cloves, cinnamon, allspice
1 tablespoon of crushed or powdered orris root
1 tablespoon powdered gum benzoin
20 drops of rose essential oil
5 drops lavender essential oil
5 drops of lemon or orange fragrance oil

Mix the orris root and gum benzoin together and put in a small cheese shaker. Dry flowers as above and toss together gently until mixed. Place a 1-inch layer of the flower mixture in a plastic pan. Sprinkle a small amount of fixative (orris and gum benzoin combo) then spray some of the fragrance(s) you have chosen. Repeat the process again, and continue to do this to all 1-inch layers until done. Put on rubber gloves and toss it all as you would a salad. Put the batch in a closed container to mature.

# MORE FUN WITH PLANTS

I have always wanted to present a friend with a plant that was started as a result of a special meal together from my house. I am enchanted with the thought that it represents our ongoing friendship, sprouted from our meal and time together …

## Avocado
Take the pit from the avocado. Insert three or four toothpicks around the middle; use them to suspend the pit flat side down over a glass. Add water until the base of the pit is submerged. The pit will crack eventually and a root will emerge, followed by a stem shooting upward. Cut the stem halfway down when it's about 7-inches tall to encourage branching. Plant in earth or a container when the stem is about 1 foot tall; set in bright sunlight.

## Sweet Potato
Use inserted toothpicks to suspend potato over glass with the end that looks like it has never been cut in the water. Keep it in a warm, sunny spot, and soon vines with leaves will appear and climb up your window—train them with a string. Do not transplant to soil, but keep water level constant.

## Orange or Grapefruit Grove
Plant seeds from your citrus fruit as soon as you take them out of the fruit—do not let them dry out. Place them in potting soil about 1/2-inch down. Water them well and cover with plastic wrap loosely. Place in bright light. Keep moist and warm while the green shoots appear. Remove plastic when the shoots come through. Keep in bright light and it will grow … and grow … and grow!

## Ginger
Suspend a 2- to 3-inch piece of ginger root horizontally across the top of a glass with toothpicks. Add water until bottom 1/3 of root is submerged. Roots will sprout first. When the roots are 1- to 2-inches long, plant in soil just below the surface and place in gentle sunlight. Stems and leaves will appear and grow.

# Herbal Vinegars, Butters, and Teas

## Vinegars

Get an interesting glass "table" bottle and fill it 1/4 to 1/2 full of the herb or eatable flower (the amount depends on how strong you want the taste in the vinegar). Pour vinegar over the herb or flowers in the bottle (use white vinegar and not apple cider for purity of taste). Let this concoction mature in a cool, dry place for a couple of months, and the flavored vinegar is ready (you can choose to strain it or not, depending on your preference). No need to refrigerate; vinegars will keep approximately four to six months.

## Butters

You can make these with butter or margarine. Soften butter by partially melting it first, then add ground herbs or eatable flowers—I like to add one teaspoon to every cup of butter for a mild taste, but you can add more. After you have added the herbs, then whip the butter combo for a minute or two, and store it in the refrigerator for quick setup. Flavored butters are lovely with dinner or at tea parties. You can also "flavor" butter with the flavorings you get for making candy or cakes—be creative! Here is my favorite recipe:

1 cup butter
1 drop orange flavoring
1 teaspoon crushed pineapple mint leaves

I make this refreshing mint butter to use on vegetables or bread.
Or how about …
… lemon-rosemary butter on chicken …
sage and thyme butter with Thanksgiving dinner ….

## Teas (Infusions)

You can buy tea bags in gourmet coffee and tea stores, or in health food stores (or, use a tea infuser). Simply load the bag about 1/2 full of the dried herb, herb mix, or eatable flowers. To make a proper tea, make sure that you pour the hot water over the bag, cover the cup with a saucer or small plate, and let it steep for at least three minutes (ten to twelve minutes for a full-strength infusion). Then remove the tea bag or infuser and enjoy.

# Chapter 6

# Functional Garden Basics: Problem Solving, Down to the Nitty-Gritty

# IN THIS CHAPTER:

## Homemade Soil Mixes
### Casey's "Super Natural" Basic Potting Soil Mixes
Mix for heavy clay soils
Mix for sandy to normal soils

## Fertilizers, Composts, and Mulches, Oh My!
### Compost
### Mulches
### Fertilizers

Fishy Fertilizer
Seaweed Fertilizer
Coffee and Berry Mash Fertilizer
Herbal Mold Inhibitor

We have covered some of the most romantic aspects of the garden, and I hope you are excited, inspired, and ready for all the peace, joy, pleasure, and romance that a garden and the fruits of your labor will bring. But now we need to get into the nitty-gritty—the basics of a successful garden, and the cures for what "ails" it.

A garden needs light, air, soil, and water to grow. As with most anything in life, expect to plan a little, and work a little, for the best outcome with your garden. But what about garden problems? This part of the book will tell you how to resolve them with budget-minded and earth-healthy solutions.

Mother Nature says: "When it comes to problems, it's not the problem itself, but how you handle it that determines your success."

# HOMEMADE SOIL MIXES

To start with, here are two soil mixes that will help your garden grow—they are both good; it is your starting soil texture which will guide you as to which one you use. All gardens need nitrogen, phosphorus, potash and trace minerals, fertilizer, microbiotic life, humus, and calcium along with natural earth. Both soil mixes are rich in most of these nutrients. These potting soils can be used in container gardening or to put around plant roots (about 6-inches thick to assist soil conditions when planting in the earth).

When making a soil mix, you need to include the following items to help enrich the soil:

### Nitrogen

This element is essential to plant growth and vigor. An ongoing supply of good compost and other organic matter should take care of the nitrogen needs of most gardens. If your plants are slow growing or have light green to yellow foliage when they should be dark green, bump up the nitrogen in your soil.

To add nitrogen to soil, use the following items from a garden store:

Cottonseed meal

Fishy Fertilizer (also has lots of trace minerals—see page 79)

Blood meal

Hoof meal

Bone meal

### Phosphorus

This helps promote cell division and root development, and is really critical in fruit growth. If your fruiting crops had leaves but bore no fruit, increase the phosphorus in your soil.

To add phosphorus to soil, use bone meal or finely-ground phosphate rock.

## Potash (Potassium)

Potash is vital for cell division, but also helps form strong stems and helps your plants fight off disease. Do you have lots of spindly plants with yellow, streaked leaves? Add potash and trace minerals (add two from this list to soil).

Kelp meal
Wood ashes
Crushed granite
Greensand
Coffee grounds

## Trace Minerals

Soil benefits from these micronutrients: Boron, chlorine, copper, calcium, iron, magnesium, manganese, molybdenum, sulfur, and zinc. These are usually available in good soil, but if you want to add more trace minerals, you can do so by adding Fishy Fertilizer (which is full of nutrients) along with some liquid kelp.

## Microbiotic Life and Humus

These contain the good bacteria that are necessary for the soil to "work" with all the elements to make your garden robust. The best source for them is compost.

## Casey's "Super Natural" Basic Potting Soil Mix

*(For heavy clay soils)*

### You will need:

6 cups topsoil
1 cup sand
1 cup vermiculite
2 cups peat moss
1/2 cup coffee grounds
1 teaspoon potash
1 teaspoon bone meal
1 tablespoon Epsom salts
1 cup compost

# Casey's Super Natural Basic Potting Soil

### (For sandy to normal soils)

### You will need:

6 cups topsoil
1 cup dehydrated manure
2 teaspoons bone meal
2 teaspoons Fishy Fertilizer (see page 79)
1/2 cup vermiculite
1 cup peat moss
1 tablespoon Epsom salts
1 cup compost
2 teaspoons wood ash

I multiply this recipe by 10-20 times (takes the same amount of time to make and I have plenty made ahead that I keep in a large garbage can with lid). Throw in a few earthworms and they will continue to keep the mix loose.

Soils have different pH values in different areas, and your topsoil may have to be adjusted to a favorable pH. Here is a simple test you can do to find out if your soil needs correction. Take a sample of soil from a spot about three to four inches deep. Mix about 2 tablespoons of this soil with about 1 cup of distilled water (it is important to use commercially-distilled water since it has a neutral pH, close to 7) and allow the soil to settle. Test the pH with the help of a purchased pH kit (often sold in gardening and pool sections).

If your soil is too alkaline (pH showing numbers higher than 7) correct by adding sulfur powder, ammonium salts, or gypsum (calcium sulfate) available from gardening or hardware stores. Add these in small amounts at a time until the pH is very close to 7.

If your soil is too acidic (pH showing numbers lower than 7), correct by adding lime (calcium oxide), calcium carbonate, or unscented talcum powder in small amounts and re-testing the pH until you've raised the pH to around 6.5 (I think 6.5 is better than 7 because it encourages some of the "good bacteria" in your garden for a perfect balance).

Wearing rubber gloves, mix the correctives and soil in a large plastic garbage can. Use a small shovel to "toss" the mix. I make about a half of a garbage can at a time so I have room to "toss" my mix. When I am done, I can put the lid on the garbage can and take out what I need for potting whenever I need it. Then, when I bring home those bargain, root-bound plants from the nursery that so badly need to be transplanted, I go right to my potting area, grab larger pots, use some soil from my "garbage can" and transplant them quickly. I toss a little compost on top, add a small layer of mulch, soak them with water and both the plants and I can go about our business happily. This whole process takes me five to ten minutes because my potting station is always ready with my "Super Natural" potting mix, compost, and mulch.

# FERTILIZERS, COMPOSTS, AND MULCHES, OH MY!

## Compost

Maybe you are one of the lucky ones who live in an area with nutrient-rich, virgin soil that will grow almost everything. Most of us, however, have soil that has been over-used, is full of undesirable weed seeds, or contains too much clay or sand. Compost will enrich the soil and provides plants with the ideal growing environment.

If you are in a hurry, you can buy compost at the store, but you can also make it yourself by "recycling" your yard waste. You'll save money on your garbage bill and your budget if you have a "working" compost pile in the corner of your yard.

## Making Compost

Decomposed leaves and other bulky, organic matter produces the beneficial microorganisms and oxygen that are the basis of compost. Homemade garden compost is a soil-conditioner second to none, improving the soil's drainage *and* moisture-retaining capacity.

The best method of composting is the aerobic (because oxygen is present to aid in the process) method, which produces great compost within three to five months. You will need a bin or box made out of old wood fencing—or you can buy commercial plastic bin composters at the garden store. I like the three-sided wood fencing (make the slats very close together with only an inch or two in between). You need to be able to get to the compost to turn the decomposing matter occasionally so that you can make sure that it is getting ventilation. Some people like to build two bins side-by-side so that by the time the second bin is full, the first one should be done with the heating process and decomposed enough to use.

To start, loosen the soil beneath your bin, and add rock to facilitate the drainage at the bottom of the compost pile. Next, add a one-foot-thick layer of grass clippings and leaves, and then mix in about a pound of commercial animal manure (or you can add ammonium sulfate found at the garden store or hardware store) as an "activator." I also like to buy some earthworms and toss a few in now and then (they help with the break-down process). As you slowly add your materials to your compost pile, repeat this layering procedure, and turn with a pitchfork, hoe, or shovel occasionally to make sure you are adding air. When the pile is getting high, cover it with plastic (punch some holes in the plastic to let some air in) and leave it alone for about thirty days. The natural decomposition of these organic materials produces heat, so this part of the composting process is called "heating." During this phase, the pile heats up and kills any weed-seeds. After the compost has been allowed to heat for about thirty days, uncover and turn to mix it, using a shovel or rake. Cover it again for thirty more days, turning it one more time to make sure that the mixture is fine and crumbly. You now have your own enriched soil additive, at virtually no cost to you. This is the most perfect example of Mother Nature's recycling I can think of!

# Mulches

If you mulch the plants in your garden, you'll save yourself a lot of weeding! But perhaps even more important, mulching also helps retain moisture in the soil, thereby keeping the soil temperature more uniform—which makes plants happy. If your planting is well-planned with plenty of nutrient-rich organic materials from the compost pile in with the soil and a mulch on top, this will also feed and condition the soil and produce beautiful, bountiful crops. Mulch is commercially available at stores, or you can make your own by mixing equal parts of compost and straw or old leaves together, and apply about 1-inch thick on top of the soil around your plant. The straw or old leaves will help hold warmth to the soil in cooler climates and give coolness in hot situations (kind of like the insulation in our homes). When planting, mix a little compost with the nutrient-rich potting soil. After your plant is in the ground or pot, put a small amount of compost (about 1-inch deep) on top of the soil and top it off with about 1/2-inch of old straw or bark.

## Fertilizers

This can be a "stinky" topic when you understand where most fertilizers come from. Mother Nature offers a surprising variety of natural fertilizers. Some herbs make great fertilizers (and can be less offensive to the nose), as do coffee grounds and fish oils. All the materials in this section provide safe and natural ways to fertilize your plants and encourage them to grow.

## Fishy Fertilizer

### You will need:

1/2 cup tuna juice (water portion drained from "water packed" tuna in tuna cans)
1/2 cup water
1 drop of unscented mild detergent

This liquid fertilizer may not smell great, but your plants will love it. The fish water provides nitrogen, while the small amount of detergent breaks the surface tension of the water and helps the plants absorb the mixture. To make it, strain the liquid from a small can of water-packed tuna into a measuring cup. Add additional water to get 1/2 cup of liquid. Add the drop of mild detergent, put the mixture in a bottle, and shake well. To use, fertilize your plants with a mixture of 1/4 cup of this recipe to 2 cups of water. Use right away.

# Seaweed Fertilizer

## You will need:

1 cup kelp/seaweed juice
3 cups water

To make kelp or seaweed juice: Purchase kelp or seaweed from a Japanese store or deli that sells the strips for wrapping sushi (you can also use seaweed flakes). Place in a pan ready for the stovetop 2 tablespoons of seaweed/kelp flakes or two to three strips of seaweed/kelp strips in 1 cup of water. Bring mixture to boil, then remove from heat and cover the pan, letting the mix steep for 15 minutes. When cool, add the other 2 cups water.

Use right away on plants, applying small amounts to soil as you do when watering plants. Seaweed/kelp water provides nitrogen.

# Coffee and Berry Mash Fertilizer

This is a fun one to make and, surprise!— it smells just fine. It can stain, though, so be careful not to get it on your clothes or carpet.

## You will need:

4 tablespoons of concentrated juice squeezed from used, ground coffee
3 cups water
1/2 cup berry mash

Make a "berry mash" by bruising and crushing seasonal berries (raspberries, blackberries, and blueberries seem to work best) with a potato masher or other kitchen instrument. The mash should contain both juice and pulp. Mix the mash with the coffee juice and water and store in a pretty container. Use the mash directly as plant water. The refrigerated shelf life of this fertilizer is about one month.

# Herbal Mold Inhibitor-Light Fertilizer

These herbs, when mixed, seem to work as a light fertilizer, toner, and anti-mold help for your plants (particularly helpful in climates with high humidity).

### You will need:

1/4 cup dried nettle
1/4 cup dried comfrey root (or a few drops of essential oil if you cannot find the plant)
1/4 cup dried chamomile
4 cups hot water

Chop and then crush the herbs. Place them in a large container. Pour the hot water over the herbs, cover, and allow it to steep for 24 hours. Strain the mixture and use the liquid as a fertilizer to help tone and condition plants that have mold or fuzz problems. (You have really made an herbal tea for your plants that tones and works as an anti-mold/anti-fungal.) This mixture will keep in your refrigerator for approximately three weeks.

# Chapter 7

# Mother Earth's Solutions for the Garden and Pests

# IN THIS CHAPTER:

## Garden

Shine and Glow Houseplant Polish
Natural Weeding Solution
Mold and Mealy Bugs on Plants
Fungus Stopper
Mildew-Mold Control for Plants
Garden Chemical Neutralizer
Natural Weed Deterrent

## Pests

Natural Pest Control
Garden Fly Trap
Natural Roach Killer
Homemade Insecticide
Aphids-Be-Gone!
Good and Pretty Bugs
Aphid and Beetle Repellent
Yellow Jackets' Death Trap
Softening Bees
Byron's Slug Fighter #1
Byron's Slug Fighter #2
Other Tricks to Rid Your Garden of Slugs
Fly, Tick, and Mosquito Repellent Spray
General Bug Spray/No-Lick Spray
Controlling Spiders
Mother Nature to the Rescue

## Controlling Larger Pests

Birds
Old Fashioned Deer and Rabbit Repellent
Quick and Easy Deer and Rabbit Repellent
Moles and Mice
Mole-Away
Skunks, Rats, Rabbits, Raccoons, and Opossums
Dogs and Other Family Pets in the Garden

## Shine and Glow Houseplant Polish

This is a great "clean and shine" product to remove the dust that accumulates on plants, and one that gives them back their luster. It's a natural cosmetic to help your plants have a healthy glow. Cosmetics for your plants? Sure! Now just talk to them, too, and they will grow like crazy.

### You will need:

- 1 tablespoon apricot kernel, sweet almond, or olive oil
- 1 teaspoon unscented gentle cleanser or shampoo
- 3 cups warm water

*Before you use this, move your plants to the bathtub or outside to avoid water messes.*

Pour into a spray bottle and shake. Oil and water do not mix so you will need to shake the bottle a lot while you are spraying it on, which is okay because a little oil goes a long way on the leaves. For delicate leaves, spray on a fine mist and follow with a fine mist of plain water. For large, waxy leaves, spray on the mix and then wipe off. This mix has no shelf life, so mix and use it immediately. Don't be tempted to substitute a mineral oil for the natural oil in this formula as it will coat the leaves and diminish the plant's carbon dioxide and oxygen exchange. The natural oil allows the plant to "breathe." If you want this recipe to completely mix, try substituting natural "water soluble" bath oil for the sweet almond oil.

## Natural Weeding Solution

Use this around the house or sidewalks where you want no plants or weeds to grow:

Dig a small trench about 2-inches wide and fill with rock salt. Activate with a fine mist of water and plants will usually not grow within a foot of this place The salt will not harm your pets if they lick it.

## Molds and Mealy Bugs on Plants

Give your plants a spa-bath! Dissolve 1 cup Epsom salts in 1-1/2 cups water. Use this solution to wash down the plant leaves. Mix a little in the top 1/2-inch of soil around the plant; it will repel mealy bugs and helps kill the mold on plant leaves and in the top-soil around plant.

## Fungus Stopper

One of the most famous fungicides in the world is known as "Bordeaux mixture." It was discovered when a French botanist named Alexis Millardet noticed that certain grapevines in France were not suffering from mildew. He asked the farmer why, and was told that the grapes, which had a blue tinge on the leaves, had been sprayed with a mixture of copper sulfate (bluestone) and lime to cut down on fruit pilfering from the pests in the area. This was quite a discovery, as it turns out that copper is toxic to the fungus, and the addition of lime both adheres the mix to the vine and helps reduce the chance of getting too much copper on the plant, which would be toxic to it. Look for copper sulfate or "bluestone" in garden stores, or look for anti-fungal commercial sprays that contain it. As a short cut, you can still buy the Bordeaux mixture in garden stores. If you can't find it—here's a recipe to make a Bordeaux mixture yourself: mix all together, and lightly spray on plants.

### You will need:

3 tablespoons of copper sulfate
2 tablespoons of lime
1 cup warm water

## Need to Clean Large-Leafed Plants?

I don't know about you, but it seems that I routinely end up with one mate-less sock on certain laundry days—the other sock just never materializes. A great use for that one sock is to dampen it with a combination of water and cheap hair spray and use it to clean large plant leaves. (Hint: You can also use other single socks for dusting furniture or cleaning windows or mirrors.)

## Mildew-Mold Control for Plants

### You will need:

3-1/2 teaspoons of baking soda
1 teaspoon of tea tree tincture
1 teaspoon of liquid dish detergent
1 gallon of water

Mix well and spray on plants and topsoil.

# Garden Chemical Neutralizer

You can "neutralize" or detoxify plants or lawns that you suspect have been chemically treated. A friend who is sensitive to chemicals recently purchased a new home. When the landscaper had finished, he left a note indicating that he had treated the lawn with a prominent weed killer. I searched and researched and came up with this neutralizer to help clear pre-existing pesticides in gardens. The detergent breaks down the chemical, allowing it to be flushed away more quickly; the sugar contained in the corn syrup also helps with the chemical breakdown process.

*You will need:*

2 cups corn syrup
3/4 cups baby shampoo
15 gallons of water

Put this mixture into a sprayer and apply; it will cover approximately 245 square feet.

# Natural Weed Deterrent

## *You will need:*

2 tablespoons apple cider vinegar
2 teaspoons baby shampoo
2 tablespoons gin or vodka

Mix and spray on lawn. This formula is non-toxic to children and pets.

# PESTS

## Natural Pest Control

As a plant lover, bugs and crawly things have never been a popular subject for me, although I realize that several of our earth's creeping members are really helpful—and even necessary. Sometimes, however, these little creatures really get out of control and tip the balance of nature, or try to come into my garden room indoors where they are *not* welcome.

Ridding your garden of pests without damaging the environment can be a challenge. I'm sure you have read or heard of the dangers of many of today's fertilizers and pesticides. Some of the more commonly used inorganic pesticides are neither people-friendly nor safe to use, and include such chlorinated hydrocarbons as DDT, Lindane, Chlordane, Heptachlor, and Aldin, just to name a few. Even though these are usually used in graded dosages, which are then blended back to be moderately low in toxicity to animals and humans, these compounds do not leave our environment quickly (some take more than a decade to degrade). These chemicals can build up in concentrations over time in our food chain and in our bodies. I could belabor this indefinitely, as I truly want to build a case for safer, more natural solutions to irritating pest problems, but trust that this small amount of information about some of the commercial pesticides does just that.

I have borrowed time-honored solutions from the knowledgeable Western farmers around me. Some of these solutions have been handed down from generation to generation, while others are "new age" solutions. Still others are adaptations of commercial products that may not be altogether natural, but are *less* toxic and less expensive than their commercial cousins. The choices, as always, are up to you. All of the following recipes are effective and easy to make.

## Garden Fly Trap

Whiteflies and common black flies are attracted to bright colors. Paint small wood stakes bright yellow (which seems to be their favorite color–although this is only an observation, since I could not interview one). Then smear the stake with something sticky such as petroleum jelly, or you can wrap the pole like a candy cane with a commercial fly-catcher strip. Place the stakes among your plants in your garden to snare flies.

## Natural Roach Killer

I like this recipe because the boric acid is readily available at the pharmacy and is toxic only when consumed. (Keep away from animals and children!) Compared with other toxic substances, boric acid is much safer to work with and yet does the job.

### You will need:

4 teaspoons of boric acid
4 teaspoons of sugar
4 teaspoons of cornstarch
4 teaspoons of solid shortening

This mixture is a naturally toxic feast for these deplorable pests. Mix the ingredients together well, and set in little balls under the sink and other places where roaches like to hang out (while keeping them well out of reach of pets and children). The sugar and cornstarch attract the roaches to the feast, the shortening holds the compound together and keeps the boric acid in the roach's system. Shelf life: approximately three to five months.

# Homemade Insecticide

## Works on most pests

### You will need:

1 tablespoon liquid dishwashing detergent
1 cup of vegetable oil

Mix and shake well. Add 3 tablespoons of the mix to 1 cup water and shake again. Pour all into a garden spray bottle and spray on plants (to the tops and bottoms of the leaves) every four to five days. Some pests have stages of development so you may need to repeat this process for a full month to terminate the cycle.

## Aphids-Be-Gone!

Aphids and Whiteflies can be a problem to your plants. Mix 4 parts water with 1 part rubbing alcohol. Put this mix in a spray bottle and spray on plant every day for two to three days.

## Good and Pretty—Ladybugs

Ladybug, ladybug *don't* fly away; stay and eat some aphids today!

If you have an aphid problem, you can actually buy ladybugs to put in infested areas. Check in garden books and at your garden store.

## Aphid and Beetle Repellent
### (This may work for pets, too.)
### You will need:

1/2 onion, finely chopped
1 garlic clove, peeled and finely chopped
1 cup water

This nontoxic spray will not actually kill the aphids, but will get them off your plants—they find these ingredients distasteful. My dog liked to chew on my plants, but stopped when I applied this repellent; he found the leaves distasteful with the onion and garlic, and he left the plants alone.

Mix the ingredients in a spray bottle and let sit for twelve hours or so, shaking occasionally. To use, simply spray on the aphids. The solution is not toxic to people or pets. Shelf life is up to one week. If you use a food processor to chop the onion, save the juice and add it to the recipe.

# Yellow Jackets' Death Trap

## You will need:

Clean plastic gallon milk jug

6- to 8-inches (15cm – 18cm) pliable
    wire

3 to 4 square-inches (7.5-10cm) of raw meat

Water

Yellow jackets can become aggressive in late summer and early fall. Many a picnic has moved indoors because of them. It is hard to kill a yellow jacket without a toxin or physical force (and then you risk getting stung). My husband developed an inexpensive, easy to make, yellow jacket killing machine that has worked well for us for years. The first time he made one of these, I laughed when he hung it in a tree, but I was surprised at how well it worked—just as well if not better than the expensive traps sold in stores.

To begin, cut a triangular hole in the front of the jug on the side opposite the handle, about 6-inches down from the top. Wire the raw meat so that it is suspended in the top of the milk jug (wrap the wire around the top or poke holes to secure) so the meat dangles inside the top of the jug. Fill the bottom of the jug with water until the water is about an inch below the cut out area. Hang the trap off to the side of your picnic and garden areas.

This is the really interesting part—the trap works because the yellow jackets are greedy meat eaters. When they find the meat (fresh or old; the more fragrant/pungent the better), the yellow jackets will eat from the meat until they become so heavy that they fall down into the water and drown (maybe there should be a fable about gluttony based on these guys).

As the yellow jackets become more aggressive in the late summer, the bottom of the trap will become so full that we have to replace it a few times. Hang one of these traps when you picnic, and you can encourage these pests away to their own "lethal" feast, leaving you to dine in peace.

## Softening Bees

For thousands of years, humans have enjoyed the benefits of bees: They pollinate our plants and give us honey, propolis, and bee pollen that we consume for pleasure and health. It is important to recognize honeybees as friends in the garden. Honeybees and bumblebees are the only regular collectors of both nectar and pollen. Honeybees are the most important of the pollinating insects, and interestingly enough, work just one kind of flower at a time. They are non-aggressive and only sting when threatened—and then they die. Still, sometimes your garden can be alive with bees and you need to hold them at bay while you do your gardening (I need to do this because I am allergic to their sting).

Here is a humane way to tell them to buzz off for a while (this tip comes from my daughter, Nicole): Place several commercial fabric softener dryer sheets around where you plan to be in your garden. Apparently, the ingredients in the drier sheets repel bees. I don't know why this actually works (I will figure it out eventually). But in the meantime, it's good to know it works!

# Slugs—Ugh!

We live in the Pacific Northwest, known for its rain—*lots* of it. After a spring rain, we see slimy slug trails outside, and sometimes even the nasty little brown thing still creeping along. A slug will use his 27,000 teeth to dine on your garden. Its tentacles house his eyes and nose and tasting organs. When slugs leave a distasteful trail through my vegetable garden, I want them gone! We do not like most commercial slug poisons because they are too toxic, and put our pets at risk. My hubby Byron is so clever when it comes to pests (remember the yellow jacket trap?) and has come up with a couple of natural, non-toxic ways to get rid of these pests. Here are his two favorites, along with some other ideas I got from his Mom.

## Byron's Slug Fighter # 1

### You will need:

Table salt

Next time you head out after the rain, take along your saltshaker. The only challenge to this one is that you have to actually see the slug for this one to work. When you see one of the little culprits, put a small amount of salt on its tail (the salt will kill them; they will curl up almost immediately).

## Byron's Slug Fighter # 2

### You will need:

Large container with low
   sides
1 can of beer

This is my favorite, because it works as a trap and I do not have to hang around and watch. So if you cannot catch slugs as needed in # 1, try this one. Pour a can of beer into the container and leave it overnight in the area where you suspect the slugs may travel. Try to find a sheltered area so the beer won't be diluted by rain. The sides of the pan should not be more than 1-1/2 inches tall so the slug can crawl in. Pour enough beer in so that there is at least an inch depth of beer. Slugs are natural alcoholics and will crawl to the beer, get in the pan, and consume enough beer to become lethargic and then drown in it. Slugs do not seem to have a brand preference, so use any kind of beer.

## Other Tricks to Rid Your Garden of Slugs

Place small scrap boards on the soil surrounding plants and between garden rows. Slugs will seek shelter under the boards and can be collected first thing in the morning. Take the board and knock the slug off into a bucket of soapy water and the slug will drown.

Copper strips around your garden (purchased in lawn and garden stores) can be placed around the garden. Slugs and several kinds of bugs do not like copper and will be repelled from the garden.

Cut up large strips of grapefruit peels (long slices) and turn them upside down in your garden on the ground. Slugs crawl under them and die (I think the acid from the fruit does this; slugs are very alkaline).

# Fly, Tick, and Mosquito Repellent Spray

## You will need:

1 cup witch hazel
6 drops oil of pennyroyal essential oil
6 drops citronella essential oil (or oil of citronella)
6 drops eucalyptus essential oil

This repellent can be sprayed on skin or clothes (the exception being clothes made from silk and other water-sensitive fabrics). This repellent is a great natural mix to use when camping, or for when working in the garden. This mixture is nontoxic on the skin, but the essentials would be dangerous to ingest; use caution when storing to keep out of reach of children and pets.

To make this repellent, pour the witch hazel into a spray bottle, then add the remaining ingredients with an eyedropper and mix together. The ingredients will separate somewhat in the bottle, so shake thoroughly before use. Shelf life: approximately 5 months.

# General Bug (No-Lick) Spray

*You will need:*

1/4 cup Tabasco sauce
2 cups water

Mix and spray on insect-prone plants, and to ward off puppy-licking. Do not rub your eyes or scratch your nose while working with this—they will burn!

# Controlling Spiders

Most spiders are harmless and are beneficial because they prey upon flies, crickets, and other insects. Spiders and bats are actually part of Mother Nature's Bug Control Squad. In the garden, spiders may be unattractive, but they are helpful. If they are in your way, they are easily hosed away. Most spiders are non-aggressive and will go to great lengths to avoid you. They do not eat your plants.

Consider installing a sodium vapor light around exterior doors and other entrances. These lights are less attractive than incandescent lights to night-flying insects. Since most spiders are attracted to places with lots of flies and night-flying insects, if you control these around your home, you will control your spider population naturally, as they seek areas with food to trap.

# Mother Nature to the Rescue!

Here is a list of plants that have natural insect-repelling abilities. You can grow them yourself or purchase the essential oils to discourage the following pests:

Pennyroyal: Can be used as a repellent for several kinds of winged pests such as flies.

Thyme: Fleas do not like thyme.

Cedar: Fleas and moths do not like cedar.

Citronella: Mosquitoes and gnats both find citronella repulsive, so it makes a great repellent.

Eucalyptus: Repels mosquitoes and gnats.

Lemon Juice or Lemon Oil: Cotton or mealy bugs run fast from lemon. Just a dab will do. Lemon concentrate is very acid and can actually "burn" bugs.

Tobacco: Several bugs do not like tobacco, but it is best known for repelling lice. It is actually the nicotine in tobacco that bugs hate.

Garlic and Onions: Many species of small bugs dislike them, especially aphids.

Alcohol: Does watching a troop of small bugs crawling over your plants make you see red? Just dab some alcohol on a cloth and touch the bug with it (rubbing alcohol works great). The fumes will kill a lot of different bugs (vodka also works great with fewer odors than rubbing alcohol).

Lime Sulfur: Although it should be handled with care, lime sulfur (available in garden shops) is a very effective insecticide. Mix it 50/50 with sugar. Lime sulfur can also kill moles and mice. Always follow the warning instructions on the package and keep out of reach of children and pets.

Pyrethrum powder: This is made from ground African pyrethrum flowers. This natural powder is effective against chewing and sucking insects. You can usually find it at garden centers.

Tabasco/Hot Mustard: Used concentrated in a carrier oil such as safflower oil, they can be used to coat the leaves of plants to ward off insects (also will stop your dog or cat from eating the leaves). Use in a 75 percent carrier base to 25 percent "active ingredient" of either Tabasco or hot mustard. When using to protect eatable plants, make sure to wash thoroughly or you may have an equal surprise.

Sulfur: repels ticks.

Vanilla Bean: repels gnats.

Coffee Grounds: repels gnats.

## Controlling Larger Pests

We love to watch the squirrels and birds and other small animals in our pastures and around our yard, but we do not want them eating our vegetable gardens or berry patches. Keeping larger pests out of the garden can be a challenge especially if you want to do it in a humane way, with no harm to them. As fun as they are to watch, they can be a gardener's nightmare.

My father-in-law has a huge place for his garden and I once asked him about his animal control method. His garden was out of sight from his house, up on a hill near a road. He told me that he has used a scarecrow, and a bag moving in the wind, but the best plan was to just plant more than enough to feed everyone, humans and varmints alike.

In interviewing several of my "country" friends and neighbors, I gathered some more great ideas.

## Birds

As an avid bird lover, the best control method I can recommend is to frighten them away. The local farmers have changed from the traditional scarecrow to lots of those fun whirligigs sold at garden and gift shops—movement in your garden is the best way to scare away birds. Another moving item can be white plastic garbage bags tied to a pole that move at random in the wind. When movement fails, some people resort to chicken wire fencing to enclose their garden. If you are a city dweller, you may find that one or two birds in the garden don't eat too much and are pretty to look at; so just do what Grandpa Earl does: plant extra to share with neighbors and critters.

Birds should be encouraged to help eat insects, though. Wrens and robins are especially useful and are among the easiest birds to attract.

## Old Fashioned Deer and Rabbit Repellent

### You will need:

1/2 cup cornstarch
1/4 cup cayenne pepper
1/4 cup human hair

Mix all together, put in a fabric bag, and hang in garden.

## Quick and Easy Deer and Rabbit Repellent

Perfumed dryer sheets hung around the garden sometimes can send them packing, as they think the smell is what everything is going to taste like.

## Moles and Mice

### You will need:

1/2 cup lime sulfur
1/2 cup borax
1/4 cup whole grain flour
1/8 cup corn meal
1/2 cup solid shortening or margarine

Mix the ingredients together and pour them down in the mole hole or in mice holes. The toxins will build up in a short time in their systems and will kill them. Store in a place "out of the reach" of children and pets.

A more humane way to get rid of them is to buy a new humane "trap" so you can trap them, then take them far away and release them into the woods.

## Mole Away!

(This will help keep moles out of your garden and will work on rabbits too.)

### You will need:

2 tablespoons castor oil
5 tablespoons liquid dishwashing soap
10 tablespoons of water

Mix the soap and oil, using a wire whisk, until blended; then add the water. Add 3 tablespoons of the completed mix to a gallon of water. Pour over mole-infested garden areas and down in mole holes. Reapply after the rain. This is distasteful to them and they will leave.

Mother Nature's tip: If you have mice, leave a hot pepper near the area they are coming around. After one bite, they will find even the smell in the area distasteful and stay away.

## Skunks, Rats, Rabbits, Raccoons, and Possums

Skunks can be pests to homeowners and gardeners when they "spray" pets and people. All five will burrow under porches, houses, or garages; get into the garbage; dig in gardens and eat your eatable garden.

Even though big dogs can discourage these critters from coming too close, you want to reduce the possibility of these animals coming in contact with your pets. With the exception of rabbits, some of these wild creatures can carry rabies, leptospirosis, and tularemia—all diseases that can be transmitted to humans and or animals. Here are some ideas:

1. Seal off all foundation openings with wire mesh. Bury fencing 18-inches deep around the garden perimeter to discourage the critters from digging underneath (they will give up before they reach that depth).
2. Use tight-fitting garbage can lids to keep them out of your trash.
3. Keep mice controlled—they are an attractive food source to other wild animals.
4. Eliminate piles of wood or junk that wild animals can take shelter in.
5. If they get under your house, know that most wild animals can be repelled from a closed area with strong odors such as mothballs or ammonia-soaked rags. To keep your own pets from getting near these items, put them in a cage or sealed box under the porch or house for a few days, then dispose of them. Most dogs and cats find the odor of these things repulsive also, so they probably won't bother them anyway.
6. If you find a critter in your garage, house, or basement, place the odor-causing agent or item to repel them, and leave doors open so they can leave. Never corner or confront these animals; you could get attacked or bitten. For the same reason, keep your pets away from wild animals … domestic pets usually are no match for frightened, wild animals.

## Dogs and Other Family Pets in the Garden

Some pets like the taste of plants and can destroy them in no time. If your pets are digging in your garden, you may need to fence them out. You can also try the "Tabasco Trick." I had to use this solution once on some catnip I was growing; my kitty was impatient and didn't want to wait for the plant to mature, be cut, and then dried, so I had to teach her "no-no" with this solution.

Use the General Bug Spray with Tabasco on page 95. It will not permanently hurt your pets, but the discomfort will teach them you mean *no!* Spray the plant with the Tabasco and water mixture: yikes! Your pet will *not* want to repeat this trick. My German shepherd puppy wouldn't stop licking my legs, and even the bitters I applied didn't deter him. So I tried the Tabasco Trick. He's always happy to see me—but he does not want to lick my legs anymore!

To keep cats out of the garden, my friend said she has put "spiky" evergreen branches between the crop rows and among the perimeter of the garden. The prickly barrier will keep the cat out and add to the mulch as well.

# Chapter 8

# Homemade Gifts for Newlyweds, Housewarmings, and Yourself!

# IN THIS CHAPTER:

## For the Home

Housewarming Gifts: Say It with Fragrance!
For the Mr. Fixit Who Has Everything
Spring Cleaning Basket
Herbal or Floral Gifts from Your Garden to Your Kitchen:
Tinctures
Jellies

## For the Garden

Gardener's Pail
Painted or Stenciled Clay Pot

## Additional Garden Gifts

Potpourri Basket for the Crafter
Byron's Slug Safari Basket
Decorated Wooden Potpourri Box
A Starter Herb Garden
Floral or Herbal Jellies
Herbal Vinegars
More Homemade Gift Ideas

It is great to give homemade gifts. When you take a friend a homemade gift, it means that you really care, that you took time to make a product or two, think up the basket or container especially for them. Beautifully presented homemade gifts tell them that you value their friendship. These ideas are just to get you started. If your friend collects owls or other figurines, add one into the mix. If you laugh so hard you cry together, tuck in some hankies. Personalize the gift to make it even more special than store-bought.

## Housewarming Gifts: Say It with Fragrance!

If a friend just bought a new home, you want to acknowledge this special time of life. Or, maybe you're looking for a special hostess gift for the friend who has everything. We all would enjoy and use the items in this basket again and again. As a matter of fact, this is my personal favorite, and I have given it more than once to the same people every year and they still love it (the second time was because they told me they used it all up … hinted they would like more).

Do up a clever-looking little basket using these three homemade products and two store-bought ones, all to fragrance the home!

Air freshener, page 19
Carpet freshener, page 18
Potpourri, page 67
Add some fresh flowers in a basket and a
    decorative candle!

Wow! Could someone make *me* one of these, please?

## For the Mr. Fixit Who Has Everything

*This* will impress him: a great little basket that he can keep in his garage, and every time he needs to clean something he will go to his basket and think of you, and thank you (this may also help keep him from rummaging through your newly-organized box of cleaners).

Cinnamon or citrus essential oil (for removing car stains from the garage floor)
Tile and Siding Cleaner (can also work as a multi-purpose cleaner in the garage for tools and other stuff), page 23
Degreaser formula, page 16
Leather Polish (to use on his leather car seats or leather tool holders), page 15
Two or three commercial handy-wipes and a scrub brush.

## Spring Cleaning Basket

Want to give a special gift to a friend in need? If your friend is planning a big event, and you know she is "buried" in work, insist on coming over for some coffee and chat one afternoon or evening. She will no doubt think to herself: "How will I manage this, too?"; but when you show up with your gift basket and roll up your sleeves to help, she will love you forever … and know you are a true friend!
All Purpose Tile Cleaner, page 13
Mirror Cleaner, page 14
Wood Polish, page 15
Leather Polish, page 15
Disinfectant, page 20
A scrub brush
A roll of newspaper and some cleaning cloths
A little treat as a reward for all that hard work!

# Herbal or Floral Gifts from Your Garden to Your Kitchen

## Tinctures

Combine 2-4 ounces of the herbs or florals into a 50-50 solution of vodka and water. Let this "rest" in a cool, dark place for two to three weeks, shaking it vigorously daily. Strain out the leftover herb or floral pulp, and you now have a *tincture*. Store tinctures in a cool, dark place, or in the refrigerator, for several months.

## Jellies

You can use your traditional jelly recipe to make herb or flower jellies—just substitute the herbs and flowers for fruit to suit your taste. Here is a suggested jelly recipe to get you started:

### You will need:

1-1/4 cups of fresh-from-your-garden herbs or flower petals. If you use dried herbs, you will only need 1/4 to 1/2 cups. My favorite herbs (not mixed together) are: Mints, rosemary, and thyme. For flowers, I like a mixture of roses and geraniums.

2 cups water
3 cups granulated sugar
1 tablespoon honey
1/4 cup distilled white vinegar
1 teaspoon lemon juice
1/2 package liquid pectin

Bring to a boil the 2 cups water and pour over the 1-1/4 cups of flowers or herbs. Cover and let steep for ninety minutes. Next, strain out the leaves, reserving the liquid. In a large saucepan, combine the newly-made herbal or floral water with the sugar, vinegar, honey, and lemon juice. Bring to a boil over high heat. Once boiling, add the liquid pectin, a small amount at a time, stirring constantly until it is all dissolved. Remove the pan from the heat, skim away any foam, and ladle the jelly into sterilized jars. Make sure you leave a 1/4- to 1/2-inch clearance at the top. Follow the directions, enclosed with the canning lids, for sealing the jars. Process the jars for five minutes in a boiling water bath. Yields approximately 1-1/2 pints.

You can add a drop or two of food coloring (I add a drop of red to my rose jelly to make it more appealing). These make charming housewarming or summer party gifts.

# For the Gardener

Gifts from your garden and for the gardener—what special treats for new, or more seasoned, gardeners. Put a gift together as a Christmas present and the gardener will thank you (as you know, we gardeners start thinking about our spring garden as soon as we put away the Christmas ornaments).

## Gardener's Pail

Small set of garden tools
Small packets of seeds
Scissors and an all-purpose knife
Homemade Insecticide, page 90

# Painted or Stenciled Clay Pot

A small set of garden tools
A small garden sculpture of your choice
Garden gloves
Super Potting Soil, pages 75, 76

# ADDITIONAL GARDEN GIFTS

## Potpourri Basket for the Crafter

*The Good Earth Home and Garden Book* by
  Casey Kellar
Ribbon
Assorted dried flowers
Powdered orris root
1 vial of essential oil

## Byron's Slug Safari Basket

Have a great sense of humor? Here's a guy's "rainy day" big game slug hunt.

- A six pack of bottled beer (some for the guys and one for the slugs)
- A deck of cards or an action movie for them to play while they wait
- An old, disposable tinfoil pie pan
- Directions for Byron's slug trap
- A shaker of table salt (in case they get impatient or just want to be more active on the hunt)

Put all in a pail (and you can plan to spend some quality time chatting with your girlfriend over coffee while the boys are kept busy).

## Decorated Wooden Potpourri Box

Fill with potpourri—what better way to save some of your garden to enjoy through the winter?

## A Starter Herb Garden

In a large pot or a long planter, start small plants of various herbs. Tie a large bow around the pot or box ("plant" one area in garden tools).

## Floral or Herbal Jellies

Add pretty fabric tops with bows, or tie on cinnamon sticks or artificial flowers.

# Herbal Vinegars

Find out how to make herbal vinegars on page 70.
Friends who love to spend hours in the kitchen will treasure these homemade gifts, from Mother Nature's garden!

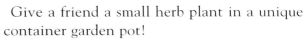

Give a friend a small herb plant in a unique container garden pot!

For an "old" friend: a plant in an old work shoe from days gone by.

For your bookworm friends: an old encyclopedia book cut out in the middle to make a planter with a plant in the middle.

For tea drinkers: a small mint plant growing out of a china teapot.

# Index

## A

Automobile maintenance 28
Automobile energy savings:
Cost-saving car facts 28

## C

Cleaning solutions:
All-purpose cleaner 13
Baby room anti-dust spray 19
Bleach for concrete walks 22
Cleaning ceilings 13
Cleaning fireplaces 14
Controlling moss on roofs 21
Degreaser 16
Disinfectant spray #two 20
Dry carpet cleaner &
revitalizer 18
Fabric/upholstery cleaner 14
Home air freshener 19
Leather clean and shine 15
Leather moisturizing polish
15
Mirror and window cleaner 14
Moss cleaner for wood decks
21
Mother's disinfectant spray
20
Paint remover 18
Pool and spa cleaner 23
Special grease spot remover
22
Tile and siding cleaner 23
Vacuum fresh 17
Wood cleaning/polishing oil
15
Creative garden containers
65

## E

Eatable garden layout 64

## F

Fertilizers: 79
Coffee/berry mash fertilizer
80
Fishy fertilizer 79
Light fertilizer: 81
Seaweed fertilizer 80

## G

Gardening solutions 66
Garden chemical neutralizer
87
Seed starter mix 66
Start with seeds 66

## H

Herbal vinegars, nutters,
teas: 70
Herbicides, natural: 85
Bluestone 82
Bordeaux mixture 85
Fungus stopper 85
Mildew/mold control 86
Natural weed deterrent 88
Natural weeding solution 85
Herbs, edible flowers:
Basil 59
Bay 59
Borage 61
Calendula 60
Chamomile 59
Chervil 59
Chives 59
Dill 58
Garlic 59
Horseradish 59
Marjoram 58
Mint 58
Nasturtium 60
Oregano 58

Parsley 59
Rosemary 58
Roses 61
Sage 58
Sunflowers 61
Thyme 58
Tarragon 59

Herbs to control pests: 95
Alcohol 95
Cedar 95
Citronella 95
Coffee grounds 95
Eucalyptus 95
Garlic/Onions 95
Lemon 95
Lime sulfur 95
Pennyroyal 95
Pyrethrum powder 95
Sulfur 95
Tabasco/hot mustard 95
Thyme 95
Tobacco 95
Vanilla bean 95
Home safety, energy savings
26
Blinds and curtains 26
Circulating fans 26
Conserving energy at home
26
Decrease heating bills 26
Dimmer switches 28
Disposing old chemicals 33
"Energy efficient" windows
27
First aid kit 32
Home insulation tips 26
Home power 28
Insulation 26
Weather stripping 26

**Homemade gifts: 100**
  Byron's slug safari basket 107
  Decorated wooden potpourri box 107
  Floral/herbal jellies 103, 107
  For Mr. Fixit: 102
  Gardener's pail 104
  Herbal vinegars 108
  Painted/Stenciled clay pot 105
  Potpourri basket for crafters 106
  Say it with fragrance 102
  Spring cleaning basket 102
  Starter herb garden 107
  Tinctures 103

**M**
**Millardet, Alexis 82**
**More fun with plants: 69**
  Avocado 69
  Ginger 69
  Orange/grapefruit grove 69
  Sweet potato 69

**P**
**Pesticides, natural: 85-98**
  Aphid & beetle repellent 91
  Aphids-be-gone 91
  Byron's slug fighter #one 93
  Byron's slug fighter #two 93
  Controlling spiders 95
  Fly, tick, mosquito spray 94
  General bug spray 95
  Garden fly trap 89
  Homemade insecticide 90
  Ladybugs 91
  Mealy bugs 85
  Mole away 97
  Moles and mice 97
  Natural pest control 89
  Natural roach killer 89
  Skunks, rats, rabbits, etc. 98

  Slugs 93
  "Softening" bees 92
  Yellow jackets' death trap 92
**Pets:**
  All-purpose cat basket 52
  Bad breath 45
  Bird gift basket 53
  Cat box deodorizer 50
  Constipation 45
  Diarrhea 45
  Dry pet shampoo 47
  Ears 43
  Ear mites 43
  Flea and bug repellent gentle shampoo for pets 48
  Flea repellent bed 48
  Fur conditioner for pets 50
  Fussy eater 43
  Gifts for dogs 51
  Health tonic for pets 46
  Healthy doggie treats 39
  High-protein bird treats 42
  Kitty goodies 41
  New puppy gift set 51
  No-lick spray 46, 95
  Pet digestive upsets 45
  Pet hot-weather treats 40
  Pet skin problems 44
  Super odor remover 46
  Toothpaste for pets
  Yeast infection of the ears 43
**Potpourri: 67**
  Floral, herb, citrus spice 68
  French lavender 68

**S**
Shine & glow houseplant polish 84
**Soil enrichment/mixes: 74**
  Compost 77
  Heavy clay soil 75
  Microbiotic life/humus 75
  Mulches 78

  Nitrogen 74
  Phosphorus 74
  Potash 75
  Sandy/normal soil 76
  Trace minerals 75

**T**
**Teas, herbal: 71**

**V**
**Vegetables, growing: 69**
  Brussels sprouts 63
  Cucumbers 63
  Kale 63
  Lettuce 63
  Onions 63
  Peppers 63
  Spinach/chard 63
  Tomatoes 63

# Also From Casey Kellar...

## The Good Earth Bath, Beauty & Health Book

In this practical guide to beauty and well-being, you will learn how to make Mother Nature your Fairy Godmother! With remedies and toiletries made with natural, simple formulas and ingredients found in health food, drug, and grocery stores, you can learn how to pamper yourself. The more than 75 formulas—including those for lotions, toothpaste, cough syrup, lip balm, and hair care-will enhance your health and produce spa-quality beauty results.

Softcover • 8-1/4 x 10-7/8
112 pages
75 color photos
**Item# GEBBH • $19.95**

---

To place a credit card order or for a **FREE** all-product catalog call

**800-258-0929 Offer CRB2**

Mon-Fri 7am-8pm ( Sat 8am-2pm, CST)

Krause Publications, **Offer CRB2**
P.O. Box 5009
Iola, WI 54945-5009
www.krausebooks.com

**Shipping & Handling:** US Addresses add $4.00 for first book, $2.25 for each additional book. Non-US addresses add $20.95 for first book, $5.95 each additional book.
**Sales Tax:** CA, IA, IL, PA, TN, VA, WI residents add appropriate sales tax.
**Satisfaction Guarantee:** If for any reason you are not completely satisfied with your purchase, simply return it within 14 days of receipt and receive a full refund, less shipping charges.